Christa Couture knows better than most how fragile are our bodies, our aspirations, our human arrangements; how resistant they are to protection, how prone they are to rupture. A prolonged cry of anguish would be a reasonable response from someone who has endured her devastating losses; but *How to Lose Everything* is a thoughtful, spirited, even-handed, good-humoured, and unflinchingly honest anatomy of grief, forbearance, hope, and healing. Expect the miraculous, because here you will find it. Expect the gorgeous, because Christa Couture writes exactly as she sings: with heart, and beautifully.

— Bill Richardson, author of *I Saw Three Ships: West End Stories*

It is not possible to reach this kind of poetic and beautiful telling of such a heartbreaking personal history without years of profound reflection and living with grief. How does a person survive such staggering losses? ... It is a huge relief to set down the burden of needing to be strong and get through everything. This is the timely and compassionate story that we all need to hear.

— Leela Gilday, singer and songwriter

In *How to Lose Everything*, Christa Couture's warmth and humour never leave the room, even as she replays her life's most devastating scenes. Is she tragic? Tough? Vulnerable? Strong? She's all these things, unapologetically, and I learned so much from her beautiful refusal to stay silent.

— Michelle Parise, author of *Alone: A Love Story*

As someone who also had cancer as a teenager, as well as being a new mother myself, reading this book felt like a heartfelt conversation with a friend. Christa Couture has experienced so much loss, but doesn't define herself by that: she is a woman in constant transformation, and writes about herself and her experiences with profound love and an astonishing acceptance.

— Harriet Alida Lye, author of *The Honey Farm* and *Natural Killer*

Reading Christa's story ... listening to Christa's words ... hearing Christa play piano ... they are all important voices in this land bookended by salt water. I can't say enough good things or write enough kind words to say how wonderful and essential they are.

— Jim Bryson, singer and songwriter

How do you lose everything? Christa Couture knows and she's here to lovingly and ever-so-gently let you in on her hard-won wisdom. She'll break your heart and put it back together anew: feeling the scars, hearing the echoes, and patiently waiting for the subtle openings of heart-bursting light. Listen closely, because she'll teach you how to walk again.

— Carys Cragg, author of *Dead Reckoning*

Christa's voice and the things that make her remarkable are so tangible in her narrative: it is bravely open, it is generous when retelling of great sadness, it is candid and kind, with a sharp and quick humour that sneaks up on you in the most delightful way, at the right time.

— Gabrielle Papillon, singer and songwriter

In *How to Lose Everything*, Christa's wry response to a friend on how to have a happy relationship is, "Avoid tragedy." None of us will avoid tragedy, but these stories are proof that ... there are so many rewards to be gained by moving forward bravely.

— Rae Spoon, musician and author of *How To (Hide) Be(hind) Your Songs*

An astoundingly generous and compelling memoir. I could not put this book down, and I know I will return to these stories over and over again. *How to Lose Everything* is for anyone who has ever lost someone; for you, perhaps, who have come to know grief; for all of us who have had to learn how to walk again, after falling to the ground.

— Smokii Sumac, author of *you are enough: love poems for the end of the world*

I didn't expect to stay up until two a.m., reading this book in one take, but it felt too important to put down. I wanted to stay with Christa through all of it, holding space for her story and her grief. She has shared unflinchingly and with grace and I will be sharing this book with many clients and friends who've been through their own hard journeys.

— Heather Plett, author of *The Art of Holding Space*

CHRISTA COUTURE

HOW TO LOSE EVERY-THING

A MEMOIR

Douglas & McIntyre

Douglas and McIntyre (2013) Ltd.
P.O. Box 219, Madeira Park, BC, VON 2H0
www.douglas-mcintyre.com

Edited by Barbara Pulling
Dust jacket design by Diane Robertson
Text design by Shed Simas/Onça Design
Printed and bound in Canada
Printed on 100% recycled paper

Douglas and McIntyre acknowledges the support of the Canada Council for the Arts, the Government of Canada, and the Province of British Columbia through the BC Arts Council.

Library and Archives Canada Cataloguing in Publication

Title: How to lose everything / Christa Couture.
Names: Couture, Christa, 1978– author.
Identifiers: Canadiana (print) 2020023966X | Canadiana (ebook) 2020023983X | ISBN 9781771622622 (hardcover) | ISBN 9781771622639 (EPUB)
Subjects: LCSH: Couture, Christa, 1978– | LCSH: Women singers—Canada—Biography. | LCSH: Singers—Canada—Biography. | LCSH: Women composers—Canada—Biography. | LCSH: Composers—Canada—Biography. | LCSH: Mothers—Canada—Biography. | LCSH: Loss (Psychology) | LCSH: Children—Death—Psychological aspects. | LCGFT: Autobiographies.
Classification: LCC ML420.C872 A3 2020 | DDC 782.42164092—dc23

For Sona, on the other side of everything

CONTENTS

PROLOGUE THESE ARE MY CHILDREN

A midwife once told me that before the first time a body gives birth, the cervix's opening, the os, whose two-lettered name I find sweetly and appropriately small, looks like a dot. After vaginal birth, the os is a line, elongated and forever changed. I liked this idea of an internal record, that my cervix would hold proof of my child's passage through me. That was before I knew about the other physical records my body would bear—a stretch-marked belly, almost quilted by the many criss-crossing lines, a belly button I can turn inside out, smaller post-lactation breasts—and it was before I thought I would want, or need, that evidence.

Now I'm glad for this map drawn on my stomach, for these signs pointing, "You were here, here and here," and grateful also, because it's easier to consult this external confirmation than to inspect that dot-turned-line to affirm the children I bore, for the proof that I am their mother.

There are photographs of my sons too, of course, but they can seem like a dream. The woman holding children in the photographs looks much like me, but I've felt dark doubt at the digital image, the glossy print. In search of a tangible present, I'll lift my shirt and run my fingers across my still-round and sometimes mistaken for still-pregnant belly—stretch marks, inside-out belly button, *yes. They were here.*

—◆—

"You have two children?" she asked. It was 2011, and we'd only just met. Our mutual friend, the connection between us, sat next to me, and I felt her discomfort immediately. I knew in that moment the woman asking had read my bio online, the bit about "after a two-year hiatus to have her second child," the bit that gave an incomplete description of why I stopped performing for a while. My friend glanced nervously between us and the woman was becoming awkward, unsure. The friend decided to answer for me.

"Noooo." She drew it out. A firm line, a tone to change the subject. I understood she wanted to protect me, but I could answer for myself.

"Yes," I replied. "I have two children."

Sometimes I answered differently. Backstage at a music festival the following summer, a fellow performer was describing her children to me, the circus of getting them on the road with her, the adventures of camping on-site. She paused to ask, like most people with children do, "Do you have children?" Her invitation to swap parenting anecdotes. "No," I said.

I didn't have children I'd had to wrangle into long road trips or whom I needed to shortly rustle up dinner for, and I thought that's what she was asking. But I was always a little hurt by the lie when I told it, even when I used the lie to protect myself. I was also instantly distracted by it—I'd start to wonder where the conversation would have turned if I'd answered "yes." I felt guilty at the denial. *I'm not forgetting you, little ones.*

I couldn't guess how many times I'd been asked by then if I had children or the similar, related question, "Do you have *other* children?" Each time I was asked, I twitched or winced, still unprepared for it. And each time, I made a decision on how to answer, trying to gauge what the subsequent questions would be, how the person I was talking to might respond. I was usually making a quick judgment call on someone I barely knew, guessing what their spiritual leaning might be, their openness to sorrow, where they landed on the hug-it-out to suck-it-up spectrum. Whether saying "yes" seemed like the right or wrong choice depended on how my own beliefs, openness and axis aligned or collided with theirs.

In a support group for bereaved parents at Canuck Place Children's Hospice in Vancouver, the problem of how to answer these questions came up many times. The facilitator, who for fifteen years had engaged in conversations with parents of dead or dying children, shared a story, as he often did, from a past member of this club no one wants to be in.

When asked whether she had children, the woman in his story replied, "That seems like it should be a straightforward question, but for me it's not." The person asking the question could then leave it at that or ask for clarification. The woman felt like she'd finally found an honest response, in that it acknowledged the answer depended on perspective, including her own frequently shifting perspective, and as well, challenged the assumption that the answer to that question should be a simple "yes" or "no."

Though no parent who has lost a child has ever thought that "no" is a truthful answer, "yes" can feel unnecessarily complicated.

Another woman shared that she always answered "yes," regardless of who asked or the context of the question. Should the inevitable questions follow—"How many?" and "How old?"—she answered, "One child, who would be five if she were still living." She didn't waver. Yes.

I wasn't always as strong. But did I have children?

Yes.

How many?

Two.

How old were they?

Emmett would be thirteen and Ford would be eleven now, were they both still alive.

Writing this is annually out of date, and even as I write it, I know I will want to return to this page and tell you again.

Saying "no" could be an awful feeling—the denial of what was important to me, the quick revision of how I truly saw myself in this world. That edit could protect me, though, from questions I was not ready to answer, from feedback I didn't want to hear.

It could be exhausting, I found, to say "yes," to say more. Saying "yes" could lead to having to console the person who asked. In their sudden discomfort and regret, my automatic impulse was to alleviate their worry.

"Oh, I'm so sorry I asked," they'd say.

"It's okay, it's okay," I would tell them, and often resent the whole interaction.

There were more bitter moments; I wasn't proud of them. In those, I revelled in the other's discomfort—*yes, feel terrible that you asked, feel terrible that my children have died; I do.* Angry. Hurt. I'd reply bluntly, indelicately, "Yes, but they're dead," and then stare while they fumbled.

"No, I don't," can come out heavy, dismissive, frustrated and similar to the above, to the same effect.

In the thirteen years and counting since Emmett's death, I haven't found a suitable reply to the question. Considering the human variables, it's probably impossible to find a consistent staple response.

········◆········

At a table with a group of people, cellphones were out and folks were proudly showing photos of their children. It was 2013, and I wore a locket around my neck with a photo of each of my boys. I opened it, beaming over my own beautiful children, but hesitant also, vulnerable to feeling alienated or alienating.

This is Emmett. This is Ford.

I wanted to leave it at that. I wanted to be connected by this understanding of what it is to love and celebrate your children. In both photos, my sons are intubated (the placement of a plastic tube into the trachea to maintain an open airway, more colloquially known as a "breathing machine") and clearly hospitalized, and that gave people pause. Most people saw the paraphernalia first and the babies second.

In those photos, I saw Emmett, and I saw Ford.

To then reveal that both children had died put a damper on the mood, though I wished it hadn't. Often the disclosure distanced me from the common ground. But I loved my sons. I was proud of them, as much as I would be if they were alive, and I wanted to share that.

Looking back at their photos, I didn't see the tubes that kept my babies alive while they lived. I saw Emmett, my dark-haired first baby, his big (almost eleven pounds at birth) body in my arms. I saw his long-awaited arrival. I saw my changed heart. I saw Ford's fluffy strawberry blond hair and his wide, laughing smile. I saw that he was happy. I saw that he was in pain. I saw his strength in his pure, unknowing baby-ness. I saw how we were all waiting and hoping.

"Was it genetic?" people asked. It was, for many, hard to believe that in this Western world, a family could lose two children without something being "wrong." I got defensive over this question, felt I was being accused of fault. I'd practised saying, "They died at different times, for different reasons," and sometimes I'd emphasize the randomness of these events by saying, "different unrelated reasons," but it was unnecessary, I suppose, to clarify.

It's not my fault, I thought as they puzzled over what could have caused such similar tragedies, piling sandbags against the flood waters of my own puzzling.

Indeed, it was the unlikeliness of losing two children that for so long fuelled my belief Ford would live, despite his congenital heart disease. I heard that belief affirmed by those around me from the time I discovered I was pregnant, that "nothing like the last time could happen again," meaning death. (And in imagined conversations, I darkly assured those people that they were right: my second child's death wasn't like my first's.)

In the group introducing their offspring via cellphone picture albums, I could feel that people saw me differently once they knew. They didn't want to be like me, and I could tell who was so afraid of losing their own child that they couldn't engage with me further on the subject. I got it. Others didn't think I could be like them, didn't think I could relate to parents of living children. I sensed some people were hesitant to continue the conversation. I imagined others were resentful of that hesitation. Some might have considered my sharing morbid. Others were moved to sadness at the thought of ever losing their own. I tried to look at only those empathetic few and resist my defensiveness over the discomfort I might have caused in the others. My mind got noisy with my defences and with sadness at my sense of not belonging.

I wanted to tell them: but I am like you, a parent too. My relationship with my sons did not end with their deaths. Then and now, my daily thoughts are full of them—with joy and gratitude for them on some days, and with grief and longing on others. Children who are no longer here still take up time and space in a parent's life.

I am not unlike you, I thought as I closed the locket and held it close to my chest.

I noticed it, the radar in my belly, most significantly after Ford was born. In Emmett's one day of life, in the chaos of the events that surrounded it, the sensation didn't have time to be articulated—that I was a lighthouse that searched and beckoned.

I could have found Ford in the dark. He slept, for most of his life, in a building blocks from my home, under the watch of the ICU, but no matter his whereabouts I could, I knew I could, walk miles, eyes closed, to find him, guided by this invisible tether between us. As long as he was living, I detected the blip on the radar, the assurance of his whereabouts, his safety on the sea.

My son's physical absence in this world pulsed like a phantom limb. Yet knowing he was no longer there did not deter my momma-radar from searching. I easily tuned into that search for a response, and I deeply felt the ache of no reply. At times, it was the most crippling pain of my loss—the acute physical awareness that he was gone. "He's not here," I tried to reason with that animal instinct that searched constantly for him, for them, but there was no changing the innate behaviour.

At their grave, with the nearness of their physical remains, that searching slows its pace. My hand to the gravestone, I reach for this additional reminder of their place in my life. Like when I run my fingers over a stretch-marked belly, I lean close to their ashes, which sit behind the stone, and breathe out toward them. "It's not enough, I know," I tell the mother in me, "but it's as close as we can get."

—◆—

It came up that I had lost a child—this was before I had lost a second—and the eyes of the woman I was talking to lit up. "I have a prince of skies," she said. She had lost a boy, her baby, late in pregnancy. It was a premature labour with complications. She described us as special, and I was taken aback. Special had never occurred to me. "We know something very few people know," she said.

It's true, I have been witness to exceptional events. I never could have imagined the love I experienced when my first son was born—how my heart grew, how a part of my being that I never knew hid within me was illuminated. Similarly, there was no way to predict the change his death in my arms would make, the privilege of holding him through his beginning in this world to his end.

The loss of two children has deepened my compassion for others, expanded understanding, inspired a letting go of little things and defined what matters most. Nothing could make my children's deaths seem worth it, but I can also feel gratitude for some of the changes. It's a duality that's hard to accept.

I might argue that ignorance is bliss, and I would have been content to complain my days away on more trivial challenges. I didn't want this insight. But I can agree, we are a special few, and sometimes the separateness I've felt from other parents is rooted calmly in this knowing.

The mothering of my sons has existed as finite, on a loop. I can replay both of their lives to their conclusions in my mind, rewind and play them again. There is no wondering what those two children of mine will become. The memories kick in my womb as ghosts, my stretch-marked belly carries the shadowy recollections safely within me and the line drawn by Ford's Caesarean birth emphasizes their shapes above it.

In 2017, the ghosts welcomed a guest.

Do I have children?

Yes.

How many?

Three. Two sons and a daughter.

My daughter was born with a word on my lips: *wâseyâw*, a light is coming. She will grow to know her brothers through photographs and stories. She will learn to say, "yes," when asked if she has siblings. She will trace the lines on my belly and know they grew in the same space she did. My mothering of her is expanding; my mothering of her is unknown.

These are my children: echoes, scars and heart-bursting light.

CHAPTER 1   SPIDER BITE

In the early eighties, my parents, on the brink of divorce, bought a house in the Edmonton neighbourhood of Parkallen. My mom had grown up on the south side of the city and my dad too had lived in Edmonton, but they'd left together before my sister and I were born in Ontario.

One day in the Parkallen playground, my mom recognized another parent keeping watch as the brother of her high school best friend. That brother had a daughter close to my age, Susan, and it turned out we all lived on the same street. He and my mom arranged a play date, and Susan and I began with the essentials.

"How old are you?" I said.

"Six," said Susan, her long red hair in two braids, her jumpsuit a pastel floral print.

"I'm five," I said, my perpetually messy brown hair in frizzy French braids and my legs sporting different-coloured hand-knit leg warmers.

("Do you want pink or white leg warmers?" my mom had asked. She was knitting pairs for both my sister and me.

"One of each," I replied. Disbelieving, she started with a pink one, and then asked, "Shall I make you a second pink one to match?" "No!" I was certain. One pink. One white.)

Next important question: "When's your birthday?" I asked.

"October 22," Susan said. I stopped in my tracks and squealed.

"Me too!" Our fate as best friends was sealed with this commonality; sharing a birthdate seemed a magical coincidence. From then on, our birthday parties were planned in tandem. Should the birthday fall on a weekday, we'd decide who got to have their party the weekend before, who after the date. For the entirety of our youth, Susan lived on that street where we made first introductions. My mom and sister and I would move to several places, but always in or near Parkallen. My dad, seen every other weekend and holidays, would move often too, and I grew up knowing many bedrooms of my own. Visiting Susan's was a fixed spot of solace.

Susan took dance and violin classes, and I took gymnastics and piano. She read *Anne of Green Gables* and I read *The Baby-Sitters Club*. She listened to her parents' ABBA records, I listened to my mom's Carole King. Susan choreographed dance routines for us, and I wrote songs for us to sing in two-part harmony. We moved freely between her home and mine, always a walk or a bike ride away. Birthday sisters, we were intertwined.

My great-uncle Dennis was the first person I knew who died. I was six and went to school that day, aware of but not understanding the fact of his passing. Even though I had barely known him, I began to cry in my teacher's arms. "My uncle Dennis died!" I sputtered, confused and frightened by the mystery of someone being gone.

My second experience with death was when my cat, Peachy, died. I was nine. He was a kitten we'd had just a couple months, but one of two we had adopted. Peachy was mine, while the other kitten was my sister's, a solution to us not wanting to share a pet. We had begged our mom for cats for a long time, and their arrival was a hard-won thrill. Peachy was exactly that—a soft orange colour and seemingly covered more in fuzz than fur. He and my sister's kitten, Ginger, understood allegiances immediately—Peachy slept on my bed and wound around my feet under the dinner table. That my kitten was the one dying was a disconsolate event in our new family arrangement. Why mine? The day he died, I rode my hot pink dirt bike to school and was crying as I locked it to the racks. Hiding not so discreetly in the shade of a playground slide, I wiped my nose on my sleeve until a friend dutifully approached. For Peachy, I felt the mystery of absence but now also love and sadness. My great-uncle had not belonged to me, nor me to him, but Peachy had. Peachy was my first taste of that kind of grief. *Mine.*

I loved that hot pink dirt bike with its white tires. I was a girlish kind of tomboy, wanting to be tough, loving to climb, run and get dirty. But I also envied the stylish, feminine ease my sister had, and I craved Madonna's "Papa Don't Preach" aesthetic. It was the late eighties, and my sister and I were on either side of adolescence. After school, she and her friends would go straight to her room, taking the phone on its long extension cord with them and turning up the radio (Edmonton's 630 CHED, *the* Top 40 station of the time) loud enough to cover the sound of their conversations, and I would head to the backyard to play or get my bike from the garage and ride slow circles around our cul-de-sac.

That bike was my first with hand brakes, and we had bought it brand new, glorious and shiny. Trying it out in the alley behind the bike shop on Whyte Avenue, I'd pedalled backward to brake, a habit from riding kids' bikes. The clerk laughed when I was startled by my feet slipping instead of stopping the bike, and I looked away, cheeks burning red. That bike was my ticket out of childhood, and I was determined to make it a smooth ride.

—◆—

Before I was born, my pregnant mother named me Matthew. She was sure she was having a boy—and sure he was a Matthew. When I was born and gendered a girl, Matthew was no longer a fit. It took my mom a few days to try out alternatives; in 1978 the top girls' names in Ontario were Jennifer, Sarah and Melissa. Eventually she chose Christa. Christa Faye. She thought it suited me, and she was right.

I have always felt like a Christa, except for a short spell when I was eight and the word seemed pointy and sharp. I was jealous of more feminine-seeming names then and wrote repeatedly, *Christina Rose*. I was certain that as Christina Rose I would embody more grace and girlishness and less of my natural tomboy qualities.

The desire was short-lived, and soon enough Christa felt comfortable again. But never Chris. Or any other nickname. When I was a child—my father would tell the story—if someone dared to call me "sweetheart" or "pumpkin," I'd sternly correct the speaker: "It's *Christa*." In later years, the correction I'd most often have to make was from being mistaken for a Kristen or a Crystal. I am more forgiving now. "There are a lot of Chris- names," I admit. And then I think to myself, *but not many Christas*.

At a summer fair when I was twelve, I found a booth where someone would print out the origin and meaning of your name in a script font on the coloured paper of your choosing. "Christa. Greek. Anointed one," said mine. I taped the paper next to the head of my bed. I still love the stories and meanings behind names and always want to know from people how their name was chosen for them or if they chose it for themselves. Middle names are often rife with backstory: there's a beloved great-aunt or your parent's first sight on the day of your birth. Faye is my mother's own middle name too, and clearly a favourite—years after my birth, she bestowed it on her first post-divorce car: Cora Faye, a soft-blue Toyota Corolla.

Susan and I couldn't settle on our future children's names, but we were clear on the details of our respective weddings. "I will have six bridesmaids, each in a dress one colour of the rainbow," Susan said during a meandering daydream about our imagined nuptials. It was long before we knew of the Pride connotation for the rainbow. "We will all carry bouquets of sweet peas."

Her family's garden grew sweet peas each year and neither of us knew a more pleasing scent. Because she had placed dibs on the flowers, I chose the second most beautiful flower I'd ever seen or smelled in our gardens. "I want lilacs and purple bridesmaid dresses to match," I said, not adding that I thought six bridesmaids was excessive.

We imagined our futures during long hours of crafting the monthly fashion magazine we invented and drew by hand. We painstakingly created and coloured pages of outfits, advertisements, contests and intricate backstory for our featured fashion designer, named Lu-Lou Baines, as well as the models we showcased. We were on the verge of being old enough to desire what we were depicting—big hair, large earrings, party dresses, breasts.

Of our many creative collaborations over the years—singing our own songs (about her baby sister, cats, the weather), choreographing dance numbers and staging original theatre productions in my basement—the Lu-Lou magazines were the most complex and long-lasting. They sustained us until we grew into shopping for our own clothes and trying on mascara for real. The Lu-Lou archive still exists in a binder, safe in Susan's keeping.

The magazine project commanded so much of our attention in part because it was a low-impact physical activity: once I got sick at age eleven, Susan was the friend who visited me most in the hospital. Home-schooled in those years, she could come on weekdays when other friends couldn't.

After high school, we changed from being kids in the same Edmonton neighbourhood to adults in different cities. She, Toronto. Me, Vancouver. She moved to study dance, and I moved to attend film school. The land line would ring, and I'd take the phone to the couch and lie back, settling in for a lingering call of catching up on dating, roommate drama, school and jobs.

But for our growing years, we were in close proximity, except for during school holidays, which I spent in my dad's charge. Joining him during spring break and for the summer meant living either at his home in northern Alberta on Jean Baptiste Gambler 183 reserve (better known as Calling Lake) or with him and my stepmother in New Jersey or New York or Ontario. And it meant seeing my sister, who went to live with him full-time when I was ten.

In 1989, they had a townhouse in Nanuet, New York, and I spent much of the summer in an armchair playing *Super Mario Bros. 2* on Nintendo and *SimCity* on my dad's PC once his workday was done. Hours of video games was not that unusual for my time with my dad. I seldom had friends in the areas where he lived, and there was no piano for me to practise on, so I honed my computer skills to pass the time alone.

But that summer, I found it difficult to sit comfortably— my left leg kept hurting. I'd adjust and shift, one leg over the arm of the chair, legs folded, lying on the floor—but my leg throbbed, no matter the position. I'd stand, stretch, rub my calf, but the hurting was a constant hum.

"Growing pains," my dad said when I complained about the pain.

"Spider bite," he guessed while we were camping at the end of the summer and he noticed my left leg was visibly swollen. "There's bugs in New York you don't get in Alberta." Our camping location was a compromise: having a site with flushing toilets and showers was the only way my step-mother, from Manhattan, would join us. But my dad, from Fort McMurray, would refuse to use them in his dedication to and preference for "the bush."

On my first night back home in Edmonton, I went to see Susan. Returning from two months away always made for excited reunions, when we compared notes on summer adventures. Long-distance calls were expensive then, and my friends and I were never strong letter writers. I stayed late and had to run the seven blocks to my house to get home in time for bed. After the run, I was in excruciating pain. I screamed and cried, and my mother was mystified. The adjustment period between my parents' homes was often tumultuous, but this was the first time it seemed to be agonizing.

The spider bite didn't get any smaller. A walk-in clinic prescribed antibiotics when my mother took me in to have a doctor look at the swelling. No change. An appointment with our family doctor resulted in a referral to a pediatrician, who was the first to suspect something worse than an allergic reaction or infection. He sent me for x-rays the same day. Based on those results, I was admitted to the hospital for an MRI and eventually a needle biopsy for what was now clearly a tumour growing around my fibula.

For thirty years I've relied on my mnemonic device of choice—alphabetical order—to remember which bone was affected. Every time I need to mention it, I think: *Is it fibula or tibia?* I so like the sound of these two bones together, and they are the only ones in the human skeleton to end with the letter "a." Their names sound feminine to me, two sisters, and I can't immediately remember which is which. I

picture facing a skeleton and see the leg's two long lower
bones, and I read from left to right—*f* before *t*.

Fibula. It was my fibula. Not the larger, stronger-
seeming tibia, but the more slender of these sisters.

The day I saw the pediatrician is blurry. I can recall split
seconds of getting my first x-ray, the lowered lights in a dark
room and holding still. I went back to school that afternoon,
a last moment of grasping at normalcy for my mom and me.
I rode my beloved pink bike home afterwards and cried for
the few blocks' journey. I was scared to go to the hospital
and more scared to admit the fear to anyone. It was a clear,
sunny day, a perfect early-autumn Alberta afternoon.

I was intrigued by the loud knocking of the first MRI
I had. The machine seemed an altar—a spotlight shone
down on it in the centre of a room larger than it needed to
be. The machine's importance was heightened by the fact
that we had to go outside and across the street from the hospital to where it was housed. As the technician helped me
climb onto the MRI bed, she shamed me for biting my nails.
"Imagine how dirty your hands get during the day—you're
eating that!" I folded my fingers into fists on my chest, hiding them even alone in the dark.

After the MRI, a biopsy. Awake for the procedure of a
needle extracting tissue and crying from the pain of it, I
clung to the nurse, who stroked my hair and asked me questions to distract me from what was happening.

The nurse's warmth, her face and her hands holding
mine are a few of the clearest moments from this time. Also
with clarity, I recall the expression on my mother's face after
the procedure. She'd been waiting in the hall and had help-
lessly heard me screaming. There were not many occasions

during my illness when my mother would reveal her worry or fear; she maintained focus, compassion and positivity in my presence. But that day, I glimpsed what an ache it could be to parent a sick child.

CHAPTER 2 WE WERE KIDS FIRST

I f you had been able to look at my calf—the leg of eleven-year-old me, who always stood second-last or last in line at school when we arranged ourselves from tallest to short-est, with brown hair that despite my hopes and direction seemed to always end up in some kind of bowl cut, whose brightly colour-coordinated daily outfit was some version of a baggy T-shirt over leggings with decorative socks—you might not have discerned anything unusual.

But when my two legs were seen together—my hot pink, daffodil yellow or turquoise leggings hugging their shape—the left was clearly much larger than the right. My earliest experience with asymmetry, a precursor to later years. The tumour was a visible lump, and the leg was a large, swollen form next to its right counterpart.

In elementary school, where difference can lead to either esteem or unpopularity, my puffy lower left leg had a certain cachet. To impress my peers in the weeks while we waited for test results, I'd push my finger into the tumour to demonstrate how the tissue stayed indented and then slowly, visibly, returned to form.

"Ew!"

"Do it again!"

"Can I try?"

It was a good trick.

The tumour was applying pressure to nerves, though, and I could no longer move my toes. When putting shoes on, I had to stick pens and shoehorns into the tip to uncurl my toes from under my left foot so they would lie flat; my prized purple suede cowboy boots became even more impractical than they were already. I'd sometimes trip over my toes, not feeling that they weren't lifting off the ground as I walked.

With the tumour wrapped around my fibula, the bone was at risk of breaking. I was told no running or jumping, so while I could walk carefully at home, at school I used a wheelchair. In the beginning, friends enjoyed the novelty— they wanted to take turns pushing me to and from class or to try a spin in the chair themselves while I sat on the side and gave pointers.

Then, the diagnosis: Ewing's sarcoma. With the results, my world shifted from the schoolyard to the hospital ward.

Ewing's sarcoma is a type of cancerous tumour that grows in bones and soft tissue and occurs most often in children between the ages of ten and twenty. It's fairly rare: in 2008, just two hundred cases of Ewing's were diagnosed in that age group in the US. On the oncology ward, low numbers like that didn't register. Having cancer and being among kids with cancer didn't feel unusual there.

When I'm asked what having cancer as a kid was like, I struggle to imagine an adolescence without it. Living in the hospital much of the time is to inhabit another world—days spent among a population of sick kids hooked up to IV poles, at best racing each other in the hallways, making crafts and playing board games, watching movies every Thursday on movie day when all ages convened in the Teen Room (those were the days of coveted VHS collections, not personal devices); at worst, and the hardest memory to bring to mind, hearing cries of agony from down the hall. Without words beyond that: knowing that those cries were from one of us who was dying.

There was a kind of fellowship to knowing that place. I gained acceptance among the kids at school and at choir practice when I was well enough for either in between hospital stays, but in the broader public world, there were stares and questions. Within the hospital, I belonged.

Rapidly following my diagnosis, the quick surgery to install a Broviac catheter was completed. The catheter was like a semi-permanent IV, a soft tube that entered my chest right between my barely there cleavage, stitched in place and tunnelled under the skin into a large artery near the heart. Its presence would save my small childhood veins from the intensity of treatment, and it was meant to save me getting blood work too—most access lines like these, you can withdraw blood from. But my Broviac slightly malfunctioned. Fluids would only go in, not out, so my arms were often bruised from blood work. The catheter's tube hung past my belly button, and I wore a small alligator clip on the outside of my shirts to keep the end of it safe from getting accidentally pulled. The few times it did get tugged were torment. I'd apply pressure to my chest and wait for the pain to pass. Every three days, the bandages were changed at the base of the Broviac, and protecting it from infection excluded showers—baths only for the months my chest bore its long tail.

Two days after the Broviac was in, my first chemotherapy treatment started.

"Exactly!" I thought when Dr. McCoy in *Star Trek IV* (the one with the whales, where the crew of the starship *Enterprise* visits Earth) learns a patient is undergoing chemotherapy and comments, "How primitive." It's a violent regime designed to just about kill a person without actually doing so, giving the person just enough time in between treatments to regain strength for another hit.

My treatment was a combination of the drugs doxorubicin, cyclophosphamide and vincristine. Nurses put on protective gowns, masks and double sets of latex gloves to hang the bags of these drugs from my IV pole and set them to start dripping into me. The drugs were to be administered in alternating three-week schedules: one week in hospital for five days of chemo and then two weeks off, followed by three days in hospital for one day of chemo and then two and a half weeks off. Repeat.

Ideally. The time "off" would be extended if my white blood cell count hadn't returned to levels that made me ready for another blast of chemotherapy.

The five-day sessions were the easier ones. I'd feel queasy and stay bed-bound on day one but be roaming the halls by day two, feeling only slightly off due to the anti-nausea drugs. The one-day treatment ravaged my body. When I could no longer vomit up the fluids, I brought up blood and bile. Every time I sat up to puke, I'd look at the clock, knowing the occurrences would get closer together. The hope I'd hold on to was for the moment those time spans would start to lengthen—a sign that the drug's storm was starting to subside.

9:30 a.m.
10:00 a.m.
10:20 a.m.
10:38 a.m.
10:53 a.m.
11:05 a.m.
11:15, 11:25, 11:32, 11:37 ...
... 2:30 p.m.
2:45 p.m.
3:30 p.m.
4:30 p.m.
6:00 p.m.
Sleep

Those were gruelling days. Three decades later, I can taste exhaustion and fear in my mouth just by thinking of sitting up in bed to puke so often. My mom would be there as I dipped in and out of terrorized wakefulness, sweaty and sick.

My uncle Ted's ex-wife worked in the hospital and stopped by during one of these shorter treatments. My vomit reached the foot of the bed and her lab coat. She still smiled warmly at me, still held a moment of care and gentleness despite her soiled scrubs. This memory of tenderness sits next to that of the nurse during my biopsy, charms on a bracelet of moments I am grateful for.

One morning after my first round of chemotherapy, I was at home getting ready for school. Running my hands through my hair, I noticed I could pull some out with ease. I froze.

I had been told this would happen; I was waiting for it to happen. But the words "your hair will fall out" hadn't illuminated how that would start. I stopped touching my hair and left the bathroom, not wanting to look in the mirror any longer.

I said nothing to my mom and waited until recess to share this newest development of "Christa has cancer" with my classmates; it had the potential to top the squishy tumour trick. With false cool and confidence, I showed them that if I pulled at a lock of my hair, it slipped off into my hand. Like magic. They were enthralled. The feeling spread.

A small mob of children formed around my wheelchair, all pulling at my head. I let them, even though the rapid removal of my hair felt ruthless and eventually frightening. I pushed them away as the recess bell rang and stared at the clumps of hair on the cement around my chair. I was the last to return to class.

That night, my mother, with much more tenderness, helped comb away the hair until it was mostly gone, the last strands falling out in the next few days. I got a wig. At first, getting it seemed like the opportunity to have the smooth, long brown hair I dreamed of. We visited multiple wig shops, all musty and catering to the styles of older women, not eleven-year-old girls. At most, I wore the wig I picked out three times—brown hair like mine, but long and with thick bangs. It itched; it was hot; it looked fake, and I was uncomfortable with my attempt to blend in resulting in me standing out. We found scarves to tie around my bald head instead, and I used two-sided tape, a piece on either temple, to hold them in place. The tape was a solution to the times the scarf would fall off my head while I was playing or get yanked by a gust of wind and I would shrink, mortified; I didn't like my bald head to be seen.

I had an almost ridiculously colourful wardrobe, purchased proudly in stores in New Jersey, far different from what Edmonton had to offer. Throughout the sixteen months of undergoing chemotherapy treatment, I amassed a collection of equally colourful scarves. My fashion rule at the time: match the head scarf to the leggings, the socks to the shirt. The scarves had sparkly silver threads woven into them and fringed edges. I'd fold the one I selected into a large triangle, roll the long edge over a few times, and tie it over my head with a hair elastic holding it in place at the back, like a long ponytail. Unlike the wig, the scarves seemed like making the most of looking different.

A shaved bald head has a short-term and imperfect smoothness—within a couple days, you'll have stubble to rub back and forth. In between chemotherapy treatments, I would grow a low layer of peach fuzz, soft like babies' hair, and after the next treatment it would be gone. When alone, I would rub my hands over my perfectly smooth head, my brow, my arms, marvelling at the softness of an entirely hairless body. I'd examine my face in the mirror; a face without eyelashes or eyebrows is quite changed. I spread peanut butter and jelly on my head once just to see how it felt: sticky, cool—invigorating, actually.

"Can I rub it?" became the request I most disliked receiving.

"It's *so* soft," said those I obliged.

Some women joked that I was lucky not to have to shave my body hair, but at ages eleven and twelve, hair removal hadn't entered my world yet. I didn't exactly understand the luck.

—

Yo Christa, get well soon!
Best wishes, Fred Savage

In 1990, Fred Savage was a Big Deal. Known best as Kevin of *The Wonder Years*, the actor was, for a lot of people around my age, the object of an aching crush. The signed picture of him was a prized possession on my wall.

It hung next to signed 8 × 10 glossies of Whoopi Goldberg, Bette Midler, Arnold Schwarzenegger, Barbara Bush and, though without a photo, a letter from Princess Diana's lady-in-waiting.

Shortly after I got cancer, my stepsister, Kathleen, nineteen years my senior, had gone on a campaign to cheer me up by writing to celebrities she knew I loved and a few she admired on her own.

As a Canadian kid living in Alberta, I didn't have much interest in Barbara Bush. Kathleen, an American in New Jersey, took it as a point of pride to write to the First Lady. Barbara Bush—or a person in her office—sent the most thoughtful piece, as it turned out. Not just an 8 × 10 photo of her and her husband, a.k.a the president, sitting on a boulder in the sun, a span of ocean behind them, a dog on her lap, both in summer-casual wear, but a letter on White House letterhead that revealed the greater thoughtfulness of my stepsister through its reply:

> *Dear Christa,*
>
> *I have heard so many nice things about you, including the wonderful fact that you sing and play the piano, as well as do gymnastics! But I am sorry to learn you are having some health problems right now.*
>
> *Your family and friends are pulling for you and are eager to help. Rely on their strength and try to keep up your spirits, Christa; I know you can do it!*
>
> *The President joins me in sending our prayers and best wishes. Millie sends a big Woof!*
>
> *Warmly, Barbara Bush*

I loved the letters and cherish them still, mostly as a reminder of the affection of those around me.

The van pre-dated "mini-" and showed the mess and wear of belonging to a large family—cookie crumbs in cracks, dropped and forgotten toys, a single shoe sticking out from

under stained seats. It was one of the vehicles that I car-
pooled to and from school in, this one belonging to Erika, a
spirited mom with wild curls and a German accent.

As I climbed into the back, Erika's young son spun
around in the seat in front of me to study the head wrapped
in a scarf. I stayed silent.

"You're a bald eagle! You're a bald eagle!" he said, teasing
and mean.

I pretended I didn't hear him and kept my gaze fixed out
the window.

"Benny, don't you know that bald eagles are incredibly
powerful creatures?" Erika said as she drove through traffic.
"I think they are among the most beautiful I've ever seen."

I kept looking out the window in silence, but I felt lifted
by her redirection. Another charm for the bracelet.

Years later, while recovering from an arthroscopy to
repair a tear in my right knee's cartilage (the medial menis-
cus), I was using a wheelchair at home, and my childhood
illness was on my mind. I wrote a song called "Weight of the
Wait," remembering that moment in the van:

> To be a bird and turn so suddenly
> To go from so low to so high—
> I would like that

When I first started spending weeks in the University
of Alberta Hospital (now Stollery Children's Hospital) in
Edmonton, the wards were divided by age. My first roommate, Katie, was from Hinton, Alberta, about three hours

west of the city. She was animated and independent, in the hospital to have a cyst—"The size of a football!"—removed from her gut.

I was drawn to her energy and confidence. She told me who her favourite nurses were and the best time of day to go to the Kids' Room, and how in the evening the more enticing Teen Room lowered the age limit to eleven and we could go in there, where the television was permanent (not just wheeled in on a cart) and the board games were *much* more fun.

After her surgery and recovery, she returned to Hinton, and we talked on the phone once. She told me she had a boyfriend, and I was in awe. And a little jealous—of him, though I couldn't quite put my finger on that feeling. Katie was my first hospital friend.

Ritu was the next expert patient to show me the ropes. Bones in both her legs had been cut and repositioned for realignment, an "osteotomy," and she was confined to bed with her legs held in braces while they healed. She, too, was energetic and magnetic. We had a common interest in arts and would spend our mornings in the Kids' Room cutting up magazines into collages.

Her legs healed; she was discharged.

Jessica had cystic fibrosis. Her comfort with the hospital and staff was legendary—she'd been coming there her whole life. The nurses rightfully deferred to her, or appeared to: she was the expert of her own care and ruler of the hallway. She taught me how to run with an IV pole and jump on its base to ride it down the hall. (Only some nurses allowed such athletics, but Jessica also filled me in on who would permit our IV pole races and who would not.)

The hospital soon reconfigured the wards, however, and rather than sorting the patients by age group, they arranged us by diagnosis. My new potential cohort of hospital friends was of all ages, which was less enjoyable, but they all had cancer. We recognized each other and compared notes easily with little need for further explanation.

Amanda, who was my age, became one of my closest friends. We started to spend time together outside of the hospital. She had a waterbed and a collection of pirated Nintendo games that meant tons of games to choose from, over my six or seven. Mostly we played *Super Mario Bros. 3*, and we bought a magazine with cheat codes at the corner 7-Eleven, where her dad would send us with money for candy. Cheating at Nintendo seemed rebellious and exciting; sleepovers at Amanda's house were great fun.

She had leukemia; she died.

Carolyn was a couple years older and wore thick glasses that made her blue eyes larger and softer. She had lymphoma; she died.

Jason, my age, was sporty and outgoing; his family came in from Stettler, Alberta, for his treatments. On the daily menu that accompanied our lunches, on which we could order our next day's meal from a few options (pasta or grilled cheese, apple or banana), he would hand write that he wanted at least four eight-ounce cartons of milk. The cafeteria seldom complied, and he was sure it was from disbelief that he could drink it all. But I'd seen it: he could drink more milk at lunch than anyone I'd ever met. Jason also had bone cancer and his arm had been amputated at the start of chemotherapy. The treatment failed, and he died.

Death, each time, was mysterious. I couldn't fathom that kids, my friends, were dying. I couldn't picture their families after those days. Who would they become without the person they loved? I also had a vague sense of the other kids' deaths intimating the possibility of my own, and that scared me. I'd push grief away to steel myself from worry. With frequency, death became commonplace. I was numb, afraid, trying to keep going. Most of the friends I made that year did not survive. New patients would join our ranks, and I slowly became one of the more senior members of unit 4D2. Each time I went in, I would notice the new kids and check on who of the patients I knew was currently admitted, who had been discharged for good and who had died since I was last there. A monthly roll call. Changes in the unit were both slow and sudden.

It was during this time that I first heard true grief—the pain of parents losing their child in the room next door. It was an experience I understood only years later, when I lost my own child, when I sat by my own child's hospital bed for days on end, but one I would never forget.

THE NEXT BED

In the summer she was a runner, she was fast
But now she's walking on her hands
From the bathroom back to her bed
Where her mind is willing living
But her body is willing dead
Yup, she's throwing up blood and bile every half-hour
Slipping into sleep in between

Her hair is wet with sweat, the air is scared and sour
She's twelve but she won't see thirteen

And in the next bed, another bald head soon will wake
To find a Frankenstein body
In her once-perfect body's place
Try to find a reason for this, try to find a reason

Down the hall another screaming call
Some kid for his mom 'cause he's scared
Yes he woke up alone, went to reach for the phone
But he couldn't 'cause his arm's not there
And she closes her eyes to the sound as he dies
But she was told to be a brave girl
And she thinks a brave girl never cries—oh dear

In the next bed another bald head soon will wake
To find that in the night, another one was taken away
Try to find a reason

Welcome home—"yes it's like home"
She says five years later
It's almost comforting how familiar
The sterile walls and halls are
Not to mention the men in white coats
Who bookend their bad news with bad jokes
They say, "You've done pretty well kid
At least better than most did"
And it's true so she feels endlessly grateful
But sometimes her survival seems shameful
'Cause she tries to find a reason, don't try to find a reason

My friend Anika didn't die. She also had bone cancer, and she had had a "Van Ness" or "rotationplasty"—a remarkable method in which a person's foot is attached to their thigh, facing backwards, so that it may function like a knee joint. Anika was unselfconscious and unapologetic about her limb difference. Her voice and laugh carried through the hospital hallways, confident and gregarious.

Inside the hospital, we kids were the same—bald, with amputated limbs, tubes winding into our arms and chests, sick from the treatment, sick from drugs to counter the effects of the treatment, tired and bored. I missed being in school, missed choir practice and piano lessons and I missed the friends I'd known for years who now seemed to be living a parallel life that I moved in and out of. But I was safe with my fellow cancer-kids, safe with the nurses who joked with us and saw us as kids first, hooked up to machines second.

CHAPTER 3 BLUE CELL

"I'm going to kiss your heart."

She meant literally. But in the dark of our bedroom, my sweetheart admitted, "I'm not sure where it is exactly." She placed one kiss on my sternum and another above my left breast.

In our bedtime chit-chat, comparing our respective plans for the next day, I mentioned that I was going for an echo.

"A what?"

"An echocardiogram."

"A what?"

At that point, my sweetheart and I had been together less than two years, which meant I hadn't yet had occasion to describe to her the long-term follow-up care I received as a cancer survivor.

Sometimes I forget that I had cancer—it was so long ago. But the check-in appointments are a kind of record of time passing, an occasion to report on two years of my life and health, a reminder to my doctors and me: I'm still here.

My chemotherapy treatments spanned sixteen months. During that time, I also had six weeks of daily radiation treatment. A mould was made of my left leg to hold it in the exact position needed for targeted radiation, and each morning, early, before school started, my mom would take me to the Cross Cancer Institute. I would climb on the treatment table in the dark room and lock my leg into that frame.

Radiation burns the skin—I had a perfectly outlined rectangular burn on a third of my lower left leg and would soothe the skin with olive oil. After the treatment ended, I pulled large sheets of skin off as the surface healed. That summer, the cells still buzzing, the rectangular shape would tan—or burn—faster than any other part of my skin. I felt mysterious and super-powered with my radioactive skin transforming in the sun.

The tumour shrank; it disappeared.

On the day of my last chemotherapy, I invited my classmates to the hospital for a last-chemo party. It was the first time some of them had been in a hospital, and it was a chance to show them where I had been for the past year and a half, where I hoped not to return by joining them full-time in the land of the not-sick kids. The land of running through the neighbourhood unafraid of fragile bones. The land of writing and singing and making things without doing so from bed. The land of hair and symmetrical legs.

My uncle William bought me a new bicycle—black with hot pink and turquoise accents—after two years of not riding one at all. I finished grade seven and went to spend the summer at my dad's house in Montclair, New Jersey.

—◆—

Summers in New Jersey are hot. As a kid from northern Alberta, I never got used to the humidity of the East Coast, which would already be in full bloom by the time I landed in the Garden State each July.

My stepsister, Kathleen, whose cool I idolized (her makeup, her big, dark sunglasses, her Bob Marley cassette tapes piled in her maroon Subaru wagon, her ever-handy tins of Altoids) and who was often in charge of my days, gave me an easy exit from playing outside in the summer of 1991: helping her paint the interior of her new, air-conditioned house.

Almost six months since I had finished chemotherapy, we were all feeling hopeful and starting to relax on the other side of the experience. My hair was growing back darker and thicker than before. I loved being near Kathleen and was happy to be working at one end of a hall while she was finishing the other. As the less-skilled labourer, I was tasked with rolling the paper-white paint on the walls, but I felt a pain in my leg each time I stood for more than ten minutes.

The pain hinted at the recent past, and at age twelve I only knew to hide my worry. I told Kathleen I had greater interest in painting the trim and assured her I would be careful with the brush. I shuffled along the ground to avoid putting any weight on my leg—it hurt every time I did. Painting baseboards was a great ruse for staying on the floor.

When climbing stairs became painful, I began to organize my days so that I could ascend or descend when family members weren't around. I hoped they wouldn't notice. My sister, Joanna, noticed.

"Do you want me to carry you up the stairs?" she offered.
I looked at her and knew we were sharing a secret.

"Yes, thank you."

I continued my deception for as long as summer holidays lasted. In late August, we joined a group of people who were camping and fasting near Guelph, Ontario. My father, my sister and I slept in a tipi, and I'd wait for everyone else to be up, fed and dispersed before I got up and hobbled into the trees, where I would pass the day with my Game Boy or a book.

At night I would sit by the fire and wait to get up from the ground and move through the shadows when no one was looking.

There was a young man at the camp my age, Bear. He was a soft-spoken lad whose big shape suited his name. Each night I watched him tend the fire while I tended my own small crush. One night he noticed me struggling to get up off the ground.

"Here," he said simply, and reached down a hand.

"Thanks," I said. We locked eyes, and first I was a little giddy that we were basically holding hands. Then in his steady gaze, I realized he, like my sister, was helping me keep my secret. I was grateful.

My left leg wasn't showing visible signs of a tumour like it had before, but it ached from a sharp point within. By the end of August, I was afraid to return to Edmonton and the next scheduled follow-up with my oncology team. In that first year after treatment ended, follow-up appointments were every twelve weeks.

The outpatient appointment began as usual—blood work, x-rays—and despite my withholding about the pain I'd felt all summer, the results demanded a quick shift into more intensive testing: a CT scan, an MRI and a scheduled biopsy. As the medical system was moving quickly inside the hospital, outside an October glory of sun and colour was unfolding exactly as it had two years before. I was at a new school; I was almost thirteen. My post-chemo hair was proving to be wavy and unruly. The school photo taken that fall reveals an awkward adolescent wearing clothes that no longer fit (but were still my favourites, so I insisted) and an enormous smile. I was so happy to be at school. With hair. And with the promise of being like everyone else again.

The biopsy this time was surgical, as the cells were too deep in the bone to reach with a needle. I stayed for one night in the hospital to recover and await the results. The next morning, I sat in my room, a small bag packed and ready to go at the foot of my bed. On the fourth-floor pediatric oncology unit, when you were waiting to be discharged, you had to first wait for the doctors to make their morning rounds and present their conclusion: yes, you can go home today. Or no, sorry we got your hopes up, let's try tomorrow.

If your room was at the end of the hall, the wait was the longest—a calculation you made on the day you were admitted to the hospital, already planning ahead to your release.

Usually the flock of oncologists, fellows and interns would peck in and out of the room within minutes. That day, Dr. Grundy (tall, handsome, kind Dr. Grundy, whose wife also worked at the hospital, a fact that seemed unbearably romantic) asked to talk to my mother in the hall.

I could see them through the glass window next to the door. I looked from them to the bag on my bed to the clock and back. At first bored and impatient, and then increasingly aware of how long they were speaking for.

At home over dinner my mother confirmed: "Your cancer has returned." She explained the only treatment left was to amputate my leg. I wasn't surprised, but I must have been shocked.

My modus operandi at that age was to weather the storm and cry about the damage done later, preferably in private. I was obstinate and wanted to be unafraid. I kept my eyes fixed on my plate, avoiding my mother's. I fiddled with my necklaces. I was prone to wearing five or six chains around my neck at once, a fashion choice I'd put on pause to avoid the hassle of having to undo and untangle them during the months of regular medical imaging that required I have no metal on my body.

"Bummer," I replied, with no other preteen language for disappointment and uncertainty, anger and fear. But also, I knew other kids who had had limbs removed and who moved with prosthetics. Like Anika, my friend from the hospital with the rotationplasty. Without looking up, I reasoned with my mom, "Anika has a fake leg and seems fine. I'll just get a fake leg too."

It seemed simple to me, though none of those kids had described the pain or the work of learning to walk again, and none of them knew what the long-term impact would be.

Adolescence is cruel to most of us. I sometimes think of losing my leg as an exaggerated version of a time when everyone's bodies are changing and becoming unfamiliar. Sometimes I think I'm lucky it happened then—I wasn't old enough to sense the possible future life I was losing, and I still had the benefit of a rapidly growing and changing body that could boost itself through healing and learning.

My ignorance and innocence saved me some anguish around the amputation, though part of that caught up with me in my late teens, when I was no longer spending weeks around other amputees in rehab or other sick kids in the hospital. When I reached high school, I was one of a kind. Even as many strived to be different through their clothes and hair, wearing a prosthetic leg set me miles apart among hundreds of teens. Only then did I realize my experiences were rare.

After that dinner conversation with my mom, I stood in front of a mirror holding my left leg up behind me, trying to imagine what my amputated limb would look like. I kept losing my balance. It was Thursday night.

Saturday, as my closest friends Susan and Dana and I danced in my basement to the *Little Mermaid* soundtrack and to Bette Midler and Paula Abdul tapes, I tried to imagine not having two feet on the ground. Susan and Dana knew about the approaching surgery.

"Guys, I won't get to dance like this again," I said.

"Then don't stop now," Dana said. We all felt afraid of that night ending and of what would follow.

Tuesday was my thirteenth birthday. I was admitted to the hospital that afternoon.

Wednesday, the surgery to amputate my left leg above the knee.

For the first thirteen years of my life, one of my self-soothing habits, used when I was falling asleep and during other times of wanting comfort, was to rub my feet together. In my adult, one-legged life, lovers I've shared a bed with eventually get used to me resting my right foot on top of one of theirs to happily satisfy the feeling of feet together. In the first hazy moment of awareness in the recovery room, I perceived the incredible pressure and swelling on the left lower half of my body. Without thinking, I angled my right foot inwards to rub my feet together. "It's not there, it's really not there," was my first thought, and my first moment of understanding my new shape. I fell back into post-anaesthetic sleep.

I recovered from the immediate effects of surgery swiftly—the amputation on Wednesday, home on the weekend and back to school the next week for half-days, once again using a wheelchair. Denial, maybe, but I had insisted on returning. I saw resuming as many activities as I could as triumph, normalcy. After two or three afternoons at school, the impact of the surgery hit, and I was home for weeks, the real work of recovery and relearning beginning.

Bumping against old habits was a big part of going from two legs to one. One morning, sitting on the edge of my bed at home, I unfurled a pair of socks, pulled one over my right foot, lifted my left stump and moved to pull a sock over the foot no longer there. The motion of missing caused me to fall over.

My mother took time off to take me to appointments (physio, prosthetist, acupuncture for pain) and coordinated with her friends and the parents of my friends to care for me at home when she was working. I became closely acquainted with the faces on daytime television—Bob Barker, the cast of *General Hospital*, Oprah—but often felt lonely and discouraged by the task at hand. Louise, one of my mother's friends, was visiting Edmonton from Victoria and brought a piece of driftwood when she came to see me.

"I was walking on the beach, thinking about you," she said. "This branch would have been tossing in the ocean for a long time, but isn't it beautiful, transformed?" I didn't make eye contact, but I understood.

—◆—

Ewing's sarcoma is a "blue cell tumour," and I wondered what kind of blue I could compare it to—navy, sapphire, steel, powder? Most often I'd settle on the image of a neon light glowing in my leg rather than that of a soft prairie sky or a butterfly's wing.

Some people gasp when they hear about me losing my leg to cancer as a kid. Fair enough: it's painful to imagine a child undergoing such an experience. But it's the only experience I know, and a limb can be replaced. If the person I'm speaking to doesn't know about my son Ford's congenital heart disease, I often allude to it by saying, "At least it wasn't a heart or other vital organ—the stuff that really changes our lives." And I have the somewhat rote reply that losing my leg was in fact a fortunate turn of events—it was the cure for my cancer.

Recently, a woman named Helen asked me how I lost my leg.

"I had bone cancer when I was a kid and they had to amputate," I said. I paused, waiting to see which of the handful of responses I'm used to hearing would dictate what I said next.

"Wow, you're really lucky," she said, slipping me off my script. I waited.

"My husband died three years ago of melanoma," she said. In that moment, I saw her anew. I saw our common ground and the gulf between us. I used to question why I survived when so many around me did not. I have come to understand I am not special or strong; I am lucky. There is no reason I lived and Amanda, Jason, Carolyn and Helen's husband did not. There is nothing in my life that is more precious or more important.

Follow-up for my Ewing's took the prescribed course after the amputation—appointments every three months, then every six. At five years, one is considered "in the clear" from whatever cancer one had, at which point the care shifts to looking at long-term effects of treatment. Chemotherapy's side effects don't end when the vomiting stops and your hair grows back.

More and more children are being diagnosed with cancer, and long-term survivorship is a place of unknowns. Other types of cancer, fertility issues and heart conditions can all develop as a result of the chemotherapy given to young bodies. I go to my appointments every two years knowing the doctors and researchers are collecting data. At these visits, I sit on the exam table. They listen to my lungs, ask about my life. They tell me my heart is still in good health, for an Adriamycin heart. A heart that beats below the place my sweetheart once kissed—a tender wish to a part of me on a trajectory set by blue cells and the forces that defeated them.

CHAPTER 4   FELL OUT
OF OZ

"Hello?" I said to an empty room. My boyfriend had closed the door behind him, and I felt it suddenly: I wasn't alone.

The sound of shower curtain rings sliding across their rail and water hitting the bathtub bottom reached me from down the hall. He'd decided to be late for work in favour of a quick post-morning-sex shower. Moments later, I heard the apartment door unbolt, open and close after him as he left in a hurry.

I sat up and pulled the sheets to my neck, clinging to them in disquiet. I looked around the room, taking in the sunlight that poured through my large bedroom windows and the shadows cast by clothes rack, dresser, hanging star-shaped lantern. Colours were saturated and surfaces seemed to sparkle.

"Hello?" I said again, and the response flooded my body: I was pregnant. I felt giddy for a moment, then flopped back into the pillows and tangled sheets.

"Shit."

My doctors had waited for me to turn eighteen before telling me the potential long-term side effects of the chemotherapies I'd had as a kid: heart disease, other kinds of cancer and infertility—chemo kills eggs. "Don't delay trying to get pregnant too long, since it's likely you'll need assistance," they said. "It probably won't be impossible, but it might not be easy."

My first lovers and partners were women. I was mid-nineties lucky that my arts high school was a safe haven for gay youth, and my first teenaged dishwashing job was at a place owned by a lesbian couple and staffed entirely by women, many of them queer. Recognizing my attraction to other women was easy in those environments. A few years later, when I realized I was also attracted to men, I remembered the doctors' caution and interpreted it as meaning I didn't need to worry about contraception.

"I can't actually get pregnant," I would say to my new male lovers.

And for a few years, despite that careless belief, I didn't.

"I don't think that I could personally have an abortion, but of course I am absolutely pro-choice," a friend once said. We were in our early twenties then and trying on our politics, finding their edges based on ideas and not much experience. Kids when Henry Morgentaler challenged federal abortion law for the second time in the Supreme Court of Canada and won, we had little concept that access to abortion would not be a given, that our easy debate was a hard-won privilege.

At twenty-five, after two weeks of not-feeling-alone and telling no one, I called the only friend I knew who had more than ideas to go on. Melanie had had an abortion two years before and was pregnant a second time, planning this time to be a mother.

We agreed to meet at her work: one of Vancouver's largest performing arts theatres. It was strange to see the building empty—I'd been only once before to see *Les Misérables*. The space seemed cavernous without crowds of people, and I kept whispering despite us being alone.

To get away from the less-private bathroom of her office space, we went into the theatre to use one of its bathrooms, designed to accommodate lines of people. I'd bought a pregnancy test that morning and stepped into an empty stall to pee on the test stick.

"Do you *feel* pregnant?"

I more than felt it. I knew.

"I'm not sure," I said through the door, too afraid to admit my certainty and harbouring the faint hope I might be wrong. Our conversation echoed in the large bathroom while we waited for the results. I wasn't wrong; the test was positive. Despite my knowing, I was in shock. We went for sushi.

"I'm planning to be at home with this baby for a while, so, you know, I'll be around if you have a kid too," Melanie said. I pictured us as young moms together but couldn't sustain imagining that possible future—I felt strongly: *I can't have a kid.*

I didn't want a child with this boyfriend. We hadn't been together for long, three months maybe. I was certain I couldn't stay with him much longer, but it had been difficult to broach breaking up for the same reasons that it was difficult to be with him. He was aggressive, often filled with anger. Both diabetic and alcoholic, he became paranoid and unrecognizable when he drank. I felt stuck managing his moods, walking on eggshells.

He'd been all charm when we met. He was the new roommate of a friend, and one day when I'd stopped by to see her and she wasn't home, he invited me in to wait. He had a clean-pressed, rockabilly look and often ran his hands through his pompadour. His laugh burst from him like a surprise, and I took his intent gaze on me for a kind of magic, missing any predatory signs. He was listening to DeVotchKa on vinyl and sipping a cocktail replete with maraschino cherry, mixed at an impeccable vintage liquor cabinet. We slid into a conversation about music. I started dropping by more often. He was moody, shifting between complaints about work and saccharine compliments for me, but I ignored the sharp turns, needing the attention.

We didn't start dating so much as we started getting drunk and making out together, falling into a relationship with ambiguity. It was messy, and Rockabilly's roller coaster highs and lows quickly became more dramatic. Very early on, I felt trapped. His next outburst always seemed on the tip of his tongue. I didn't believe his smooth talk or apologies anymore, but I was unnerved to the point of inaction. I knew I wanted out; that I didn't want to be tied to him forever through a child was a foregone conclusion. I also didn't think he should parent. At least, I didn't want to parent with him.

What a dumb mistake I had made by getting pregnant. I felt guilt and shame for not using a condom. I'd been careless, and I knew it.

I wavered briefly. I thought: If I kept the baby, I could leave the province and change my name. A fantasy I had no idea how to execute. I thought: Even if I kept it, how could I possibly parent alone, especially with my disability? Having only one leg, I had a hard time doing laundry on my own. I couldn't picture myself as physically capable of caring for an infant. I thought: There's so much else I want to do right now.

During my years of believing that I was effectively infertile, I'd never imagined myself a mother. The idea was foreign. I was working at a documentary production company but had been secretly taking guitar lessons and writing more and more songs. The future I envisioned was shifting from a career in film and television to a career as a singer-songwriter—recording an album and going on tour. Though I wasn't being very deliberate about making that change happen.

"I can come with you, if you decide not to keep it." Melanie shook me from my thoughts, and I looked at her. She sensed how I was leaning.

Melanie told me more about her abortion, in frank terms. It had been so difficult that the decision to continue with her current unplanned pregnancy was in part so as not to go through the pain of an abortion again. It had felt like a lose-lose decision for her, and she had been reluctant to accept motherhood.

I put down my chopsticks, beginning to wrap my head around the choice. My shock was shifting to clarity, the kind that twists a knot in your stomach.

On Friday nights, my favourite doctor worked at the drop-in clinic I relied on. I had already coined my visits there as "ICMD"—inappropriate crush on my doctor. Any medical concern I had was tempered by the small delight of seeing him.

"Why don't you ask him out?" Melanie had said.

"Because I have a boyfriend—"

"Who's awful to you and who you're breaking up with."

"Because what if he says no?"

She'd considered it and come to a simple conclusion. "If he says no, you can never go back there. If he says yes, you probably can also never go back there."

"Like: 'So, two things: I need an abortion and I'm wondering if you want to get a drink sometime'?"

We'd erupted in laughter. In the walk-in clinic waiting room, thinking of that conversation helped alleviate my anxiety over what I was about to say.

"I want an abortion," I told the doctor when it was my turn to see him. "I think," I added, out of discomfort.

The doctor was kind. He listened closely and watched me as I spoke. He never rushed you, even on the busiest nights in the clinic, though I'd learned that Friday nights were the slowest and he often had time to chat more than usual. I wondered if I was blushing, if my ICMD was showing.

"Women get pregnant, it happens," he said as I started to express my guilt about the non-existent birth control. "Honestly, it's one of the things I deal with most here."

He gave me information on the abortion clinics in Vancouver and encouraged me to come see him again if I needed to talk. He sat back in his wheelchair, his hands folded, waiting for me to stand and exit the room. I sat still.

"I feel its presence. I felt it from the start. Like this," I blurted, waving my hands around the top of my head. That's what being pregnant felt like: a halo.

He paused and smiled, indifferent. "It's just a clump of cells at this point."

I smiled too and tried to believe it was "just" anything.

"Right, a clump of cells."

Melanie came with me to the first appointment at the abortion clinic. In the waiting room, we cracked more bad jokes at my expense.

"Christa, it's a clump of cells at this point," she mimicked in the most seductive tone she could muster. Our joking led to fits of giggles, amplified by my nervousness. I looked around at the other women in the waiting room, hoping our laughter was seen for what it was—a way of breaking tension—and not as insensitive.

In the examination room, a brief conversation with a social worker on my reasons and whether I had considered all my options. A nurse then talked me through the steps: I would come back for an injection, a type of chemotherapy that would halt the growth of the embryo. I'd be given a prescription for a pill to insert vaginally twenty-four hours later that would "induce miscarriage."

"Some women experience mild cramping, though for some it's more severe. You may also experience vomiting." A straightforward and, as it turned out, inadequate prediction.

The nurse pushed across the table a handful of pamphlets in soft colours with checklists and the range of side effects in point form. At the front desk, I made an appointment to return, and Melanie and I walked to the elevator in silence, our levity discharged.

—◆—

I considered not telling Rockabilly. But out of frustration at bearing the considerable bulk of the consequences, I decided I wanted him to pay for part of the cost. That expense, at least, could be a shared responsibility. I found him at his apartment.

"Before you say anything, let me finish talking," I said. Roommates occupied the living room and kitchen, so we had retreated to his bedroom, which was just the size of his bed. He lay on his side and I sat, wishing I could deliver the news somewhere else.

"I'm pregnant—"

His eyes widened.

"And I've already decided to have an abortion. I have all the information."

His eyes widened further—with relief. He slowly nodded. "Oh, I ... um. Wow. Did you, or—wait. That would have been a cute kid, though," he said finally.

I felt uneasy in my belly, the clash of bracing to be either admonished or wooed with sweet words. His grand, supposedly romantic gestures seemed like a kind of contract against me speaking up. *That silent treatment I gave you? That kick under the table when I didn't like what you were saying? Look at this sushi boat I made to look like a pirate ship! You can't be mad at me now.* Erasure.

This time he said nothing further. No questions asked, no concern. He was cold, shifting into one of his moods of disgust with me.

"I could use help with the cost, if we could maybe split it. And I don't have anyone to come with me to the next appointment," I added, with a growing regret about involving him at all. I needed to leave without rocking the boat, and I thought it again: I wouldn't want to see him in my child. I didn't want to see him anywhere.

He agreed to split the cost, but without a pause to consider my second request, he said, "I can't get the time off work." He worked in catering and was certain they couldn't spare him for a few hours.

He stood, opening his bedroom door, and shrugged when we made eye contact.

The plan was in place. I was going to have a "medical miscarriage": a shot of Methotrexate at the clinic and a prescription for two Misoprostol tablets that I'd administer at home. I was all too familiar with chemotherapies, and choosing one after a childhood of being pummelled by the stuff was painfully ironic.

I went alone to the appointment. In the waiting room, I felt wordless and lightheaded.

The injection in my arm. The prescription in hand. Another pamphlet outlining the range of side effects. And done. The sequence was quick, and I left the clinic in a daze. I returned to my car and made it just a few blocks before pulling over. The daze lifted, and I started to sob. Uncontrollably. Desperately. I called Melanie at work, and when she didn't answer, I left a distraught message. I called my work friend Aynsley at the office.

"I just had an abortion."

"What? Sweetie. Where are you?"

I was close by.

"Meet me in the park."

It was September in Vancouver. Warm, bright, green. The kind of Vancouver day that inspired my oft-told joke that the city was like a bad ex: They bring you flowers once, and you forget the months of dark days.

Seated together on the grass in the shade of the trees, I told Aynsley every step of the process. She listened and nodded. She told me about a friend who was a single mom, how hard it was. The multiple bus trips from home to daycare to work and back in reverse. "It's possible to be a single mom, of course, but it really is difficult, I think."

She told me of another friend who had had an abortion and hadn't confided in anyone until after. "I imagine it must be very lonely to go through it by yourself." She said she was glad I'd called.

I had always looked up to Aynsley. She was older, born and raised in Vancouver, where I'd lived only a few years, and she seemed cultured in a way I envied—she knew good wine and the right restaurant for any occasion and the best bakery in any given neighbourhood for a birthday cake. She had a tight-knit group of friends who seemed wonderfully intertwined, supportive and celebratory. Her heritage-building-turned-loft-apartment was in a former candy factory. A few years earlier, I had announced a dream I had of moving to the UK for a year. A few colleagues at the production company, my boss especially, scoffed that I would be recklessly abandoning a promising career in television. Aynsley, however, came in the next day and placed a small Union Jack in the cup that held pens on my desk. "Just a friendly reminder of where you're going," she said.

"The thing is," she said now in the park, "your life would have been beautiful and hard with a baby, and it will be beautiful and hard without one."

"The thing is," I echoed as I tugged at blades of grass, "I'm choosing *not* to do something, but I'm not sure what it is I want to do instead."

"Didn't you want to make an album?"

I *had* gone to England for a year. The Union Jack on my desk had proven a steadfast inspiration, and I'd returned to Canada teeming with new songs and a sense of being reinvented. When I left, I was a production coordinator on World War II documentaries and cooking shows, writing songs in my time off that I wasn't ready for anyone to hear. When I came back, I was a musician. I could say it with confidence. I'd had my first and many subsequent gigs in London and returned with posters and stories of singing in bars as proof. But I'd quickly fallen back into my routines in Vancouver—returned to my job with the production company, didn't try very hard to book any gigs and was writing songs less often.

"I did want to make an album," I said to Aynsley. "I do."

The toilet was next to the window at the end of our long, thin bathroom with its high ceilings and claw-foot tub. My roommate and dear friend, David, and I had only recently moved into the second-floor heritage gem. I rested my hand on the seat for balance while I squatted to insert the two tablets of Misoprostol into my vagina. I looked up at the grey sky outside and grimaced with discomfort.

David was home, and Rockabilly had come over after work. I didn't tell him about my afternoon, my conversation with Aynsley or the comfort she'd given me. Rockabilly wouldn't sit down, was pacing in and out of rooms or lingering in doorways. He'd sigh, run his hands through his hair and resume pacing. I started to wish he wasn't there.

It didn't take long for the cramping to start or to intensify. In the bathroom, diarrhea and vomiting. In my bedroom, shaking with the chills. I was thrust into pain.

"How long does it take?" asked Rockabilly from the foot of my bed.

"Sweetheart, I'll make you some tea," said David, who squeezed my hand and strode past Rockabilly, shooting him a cold look. David was newly back in town after not-the-first and not-the-last breakup with his boyfriend in Montreal and had been patient but watchful of my new boyfriend.

I was spotting a little, but nothing substantial had passed, nothing like I'd been told to anticipate. All side effects and no effect yet.

David held my hair as I puked. He sat by my bed. I cried in pain and dipped into delirium. I looked around the room for that presence I had felt so strongly. "Hello?"

Nothing. The shadows behind my wardrobe remained motionless; David and Rockabilly seemed shadows too. We spent hours like this. The trips to the bathroom became less frequent. Closer to midnight, the shaking started to subside. I felt ravaged, beaten from the inside, and still no large clots or tissue had passed. How could such turmoil not have thrown the pregnancy from me?

"You'll have to take a second dose," said my favourite doctor, who thankfully was working the next day. I didn't feel any blush of my ICMD this time.

"I can't go through that again," I said, pleading. "Really, I can't."

"I'm so sorry it was that rough a reaction. It just is for some women. It should be a little easier with the second dose," he said and explained that if the tissue hadn't passed yet, I had to give it another try. "Do you have support?" His tone was gentle.

"Yes. Sort of. My friend, and my boyfriend ..." I trailed off, wanting to tell him that the night before, said boyfriend had slept next to me facing the wall, that he had recoiled when I touched my hand to his back to ask for comfort after the failed attempt to abort a pregnancy we had made together. I wanted the doctor's kindness to expand and come home with me, a layer of protection.

"Good," he said. He smiled and sat upright to signal the end of our visit. "Good luck."

I went home like I was preparing for a storm, readying my will and my body.

David and I picked a movie to watch, *If Lucy Fell*, as a means of battening down the hatches. We put the kettle on and piled our coziest blankets on the couch.

Rockabilly was tense, coming and going from the room but also the apartment, saying he needed to walk, he needed to pop back home. When he joined us in the living room, he stood behind the couch.

"Sarah Jessica Parker is so annoying," he said. He was upset, and I wanted to calm him.

"I'm not feeling as bad today as I did yesterday," I said.

"What a relief," he said, rolling his eyes. Clearly, I was missing the point.

On this second evening, there was no puking, no dizzy sweating. Just a slow, constant but mild cramping and the ache of aftermath. And on this second evening, it happened. Dilation, contraction, ejection.

"It worked," I said, my hand on the wall after another trip to the bathroom.

"Okay," said David with an exhale full of love.

"I think I just want to go to bed."

"Of course," said David.

"Now?" demanded Rockabilly.

He reluctantly joined me in my room. "Who picks a movie to watch without asking everyone who has to watch it?" he snapped.

"I didn't think it mattered, we—"

"You've ignored me all night!"

"I'm not feeling well with this whole thing and—"

"How socially inept are you?"

He was yelling in the dark. I had my hands up in the air, fending off metaphorical punches as I tried to talk him down.

"Shh, I'm sorry, it's okay ..."

"What's wrong with you?" He flopped to face the wall once again, still seething.

"I'm sorry," I said again. I had to pee, but I knew if I left the room he would be enraged. I tried to lie still; I tried to contain my pain and my sadness. I wanted sleep to come and the hours to pass so he would get up and leave in the morning.

"How was your night?" David asked me in the kitchen the next day, once Rockabilly had gone, taking a houseful of tension with him. The kitchen still smelled slightly of paint, the buttercup yellow we'd painted it after moving in. The big south-facing window filled the room with light. I shook my head slowly.

"I was standing outside your door, sweetheart. I just about came in," he said.

I went to the office but did little work that day, staring at the computer screen or out the window.

At home that evening, I found a tin can on a string at my doorstep. My name was written large on a tag attached to it. I picked up the string; it trailed around the building to the end of the block, turned the corner and went up the hill as far as I could see, though I guessed where its other end was tied: a few blocks farther at Rockabilly's house. Another one of his grand gestures.

In the can, a note: "I'm sorry. Call me."

I held the tin can up to my mouth and said, "No," before throwing it in the bushes and climbing the stairs inside.

—◆—

"In our culture, children are a gift. You never say no to a gift," my father said, speaking of our Cree culture. I'd called him the day after the medical miscarriage at home; he was a traditional healer, and I wanted help with the pain I was still in.

I was hit with guilt that was at the ready: *It's too late, Dad.* Also, with resentment: *Thanks a lot.*

"Christa?" My stepmother was now on the phone. "Your dad's gone to his pipe. You'll be okay," she said. My dad had gone to pray, to "work on it," as he would say.

His statement about children haunted me. I didn't ask him about it again, and he died three years later.

I carried his words like stones. Fourteen years after the abortion, eleven since my dad's death, I asked an Elder about the teaching as we sat in an office in East Toronto. At our feet, a small space heater whirred. Bare February branches scratched the window. She kept her gaze on the wall as she listened. I hadn't planned to talk about the abortion; I hadn't thought it mattered much. How could it matter in comparison to the deaths of my children that followed? But we had begun to talk about my sons, and when she asked what came before them, I remembered.

"My dad said children are a gift, and you never say no to a gift. I feel like I screwed up," I said, choking on the words.

"It's true, children are gifts," she said and paused. "Tell me, what happened after the abortion?"

"I left my abusive boyfriend."

"What else?"
"I made music."

Heya
thanks for the kind words.
sounds good

That was it. A three-line email in reply to the one I'd taken painstaking hours to write. I would learn soon this was typical taciturn style from Futcher, the producer I'd reached out to.

He'd produced the Be Good Tanyas' record *Blue Horse*, which, in East Vancouver, was legendary and beloved.

I couldn't believe you could just write a person and ask if they might want to make an album with you. But I did. And he said, "Sounds good."

Five months after my sunlit conversation in the park with Aynsley, five months from the day an injection had rerouted my life, I went into the studio to record my first full-length album: thirteen songs written about every heartache I knew by that point. Thirteen songs about having had cancer as a kid, about coming out as queer, about moving to England, about having an abortion. Songs from the first half of my twenties—a bundle of coming of age, encapsulated in the title track, "Fell Out of Oz."

We'd start each day on the stoop of the Smiling Buddha Enjoyment Complex studio, where Futcher would smoke and we'd talk about the day ahead. We spent nine days recording in a sweet, leisurely process I didn't realize then to be exceptional. I've loved the process of making every album since, but there was magic in that first time, in the alchemy of the people gathered, in the unusually warm late-winter weather.

In the Elder's office, I looked at my fingers and through them to the whirring space heater at our feet.

"What else?" she said again.

"After the abortion, I made an album," I said. I told her how badly I'd needed my decision to end the pregnancy to feel worthwhile. I hadn't wanted to give up, I told her. I'd hustled for gigs, networked with musicians, practised diligently, saved money for a beautiful new guitar. Making "Fell Out of Oz" had changed everything for me and started my career in music.

"*Those* are the gifts that child gave you," she said. She spoke more slowly with each word. "You didn't say no to the gifts."

I began to cry.

"Children are a gift, it's true. I think your dad just got the message twisted a little," she said and then repeated, "You didn't say no."

I felt a rush of forgiveness and gratitude. I'd never thought to thank that pregnancy for the path it set me on, because I'd been so busy feeling guilty about it. I'd been grateful for access to an abortion, for the opportunity to make a choice, but now, for the first time, I was grateful for the event in its entirety.

In the days and weeks after the abortion, I'd struggled. Having broken up with Rockabilly, I felt like I was looking at my surroundings in a new light, but the chain of events was a heavy weight in my body. I dragged myself out of bed, I slumped at work, I cried at night.

"Did you name it? Or imagine if it was a girl or boy?" Melanie asked over tea in her kitchen. "I wrote letters to mine, and it helped a lot. Or you could write a song."

"I call her Miette."

I walked home from Melanie's house, the few blocks across Commercial Drive and down the hill to my apartment against the backdrop of restaurants filling with their evening clientele and downtown's skyline standing in the orange and purple of sunset. I knew these scenes intimately; this neighbourhood had been my home for a while.

Our apartment door opened at the end of a long hallway. "Hello?" I called down the corridor. No reply confirmed that David was out. Still, I hung my coat and keys by the door carefully and walked down the hall alert, half-expecting to see someone. I reached my bedroom and stood at the door, still looking for a presence. My hand intuitively came to rest on my lower belly.

I was alone.

CIRCUITRY (FOR MIETTE)

What's this growing inside her?
Messing with her circuitry
That one day will be standing beside her
With the right to know
She took the long way through the night to her heart
To pose a question: can she play this part?
And from the dark, the reply: no

No, I can't make it through the wild
Leave me tangled and save my child

She's running now to the water
To wash away the hands of your father
To wash away you
But no matter what she tries she can't seem to
You're a runway and she'll never come to land
She'll keep on circling 'til she's crashing on foreign sand
But try to understand—we all just do the best we can

And I can't make it through the wild
Leave me tangled and save my child

Give me time, I will come and find you
You will always be my baby

What's this growing inside me?
Messing with my circuitry?
That one day will be standing beside me
With the right to know

CHAPTER 5   A TRAVELLER

Summer was at its peak when we met. I was leaning on one of the logs that dot the beaches of Vancouver, soaking up sun and conversation with friends, when two people came to join us. They were backlit as I watched them walk towards us, Huz's face coming clear only as they said hello. He was golden in the sunlight, and so was I. My body cast a line, a hook into him from the moment I saw him; I remained aware of his presence from that day on.

"Is it too soon to hang out again?" he wrote the morning after our first solo hang. After we met on the beach, we'd run into each other at a few other group events, and it took time to find an excuse for just the two of us to do something. No one used the word "date."

"No! I'm making banana bread, if you want to come over," I replied, not bothering to disguise my eagerness or my is-that-uncool Saturday activity. He arrived, stashed his bicycle on my patio and came in carrying a bag of rye flour. He wore a vest with a tree he'd drawn in Sharpie on the back, a T-shirt with a floral patch he'd sewn on and pants he'd cut below the knee in a large Peter Pan zigzag. His smile shone.

"For your baking needs," he said, blushing and laughing a little. I held the bag of flour, feeling its heaviness in my hands and the buzzing butterflies in my stomach at the gesture. In the kitchen, we talked excitedly, jumping between topics, trying to fit in every question and answer, never finishing either. As he spoke, I took him in: dishevelled blond hair, round eyes, thick strong cyclist legs, calloused artist hands. I vibrated with each detail but couldn't tell if we were delighted friends or more.

For our first kiss, Huz was outside and I was in. He'd been leaving through the sliding patio door. We hugged goodbye and I squeezed his hand, my own feet still on the carpet of my living room—a squeeze to tell him what I was thinking or maybe ask him if he agreed. He did.

"I feel like a laughing Buddha," he messaged later. His feelings more often expressed in writing than in person, over the years.

"Me too."

We'd been dating for a month when Huz went on a long-planned road trip across the country. So early in our fast falling in love, we pained at the time apart. He mailed me postcards. I cheered every time my phone rang and ran to its perch on the wall to see if it was him. We talked and giggled like teenagers. Our conversations never ended, skipping from one topic to the next. We emailed drunk on love. He wrote and illustrated a short story about limb loss, enamoured with and intrigued by my difference. Every email, postcard, phone call—his astute attention, his easily expressed affection, his intricate reflections—made me feel like I was being coloured in on a black and white page. It felt like incredible luck, and I couldn't quite believe it. I wrote my first requited love song:

She was cold lying on his bedroom floor
The autumn window was open
The air marching to frozen
Other than her skin she was warm
Because the boy that lay beside her
His light was burning golden

It seems her sad story could be over on this page
If she takes this painter for a lover, her story will change
She puts the brush in his hand, leans into him, says:
"Paint me a kiss, and then paint me a kiss again"

The lyrics and melody came to me in a Value Village parking lot. Grinning, I let the words pour from me like it was a song I was remembering but had always known.

"Oh, his voice is gentle!" Susan giggled when she first heard Huz speaking in the background over the phone. It was a weekend afternoon, soon after Huz had returned from his road trip. He and I had had a new-lovers kind of morning of talking, kissing, sex, snoozing, waking, talking, kissing, saying repeatedly, "I'm going to get up and shower" but never really meaning it.

"I imagined a deeper voice from his picture," Susan said.

"Because of the beard?"

"Exactly. He looks so woodsy." Already married (and not with six rainbowed bridesmaids clutching sweet peas as her childhood self had schemed, but with two bridesmaids carrying autumn leaves), Susan was always delighted to hear about my latest romantic interest.

"Is he *the one?*" she asked, still laughing and knowing I'd laugh too, with him in earshot.

"I think so," I said. Huz was pulling a book from the shelf, his round blue eyes scanning the chapters, his rough sculptor fingers flipping the pages. He'd often start reading a book somewhere in the middle and not always continue to the end. Every time I looked at him, I loved him more.

Five months into the relationship, we decided he'd move in with me. I was living on my own by now, in an East Van housing co-op.

"You're here every night anyway," I said.

"True," he said, hand on my back.

"Gilbert likes you," I noted of my cat. My cat did not like everyone.

"And I like Gilbert." It was settled. We lay in bed and discussed where Huz's books and computer would go—he owned little else and had been keeping his clothes in a filing cabinet at the house he shared with five others. We began to imagine and plan our lives intertwined.

Before we could move his boxes in, our imagining got a kick in the pants: a pregnancy test proved positive. That day, we drove to Lighthouse Park in West Vancouver, a place where you climb up and down hillside, through trees and brush before you crash onto your reward: a view of the sea without a hem of the cityscape.

It was less than eighteen months since I'd had the abortion, and just one month since *Fell Out of Oz* had come out. I was about to go on my first tour. I was newly in love and newly making strides in my career.

I didn't want to be pregnant. I didn't want to have another abortion. We stared at the ocean as I tried to fathom the decision.

Here we go again, the same predicament
I was in not long ago
And we're all just walking spirals from the inside out
Getting further from the point
Less certainty, more doubt
This boat I'm in is sinking
But I'm saying I'm smooth sailing
Because I'm afraid to swim
We're all just doing laps, getting closer to the edge
Where we find out that we're trapped
And this is all there is
The same decisions to be made
The same outcome to be weighed
We're just trying to stay on track and carry what we can
Without breaking our backs or breaking what began

At the walk-in clinic that afternoon, I perched on the table, legs dangling, while Huz sat on the only available chair. Dr. ICMD had since left the practice, and a new doctor I hadn't met before came in. "How can I help you today?"

"I'm five weeks pregnant, and I haven't decided if I want to keep it yet," I said. "But I started spotting last night and I'm not sure if I should be worried."

"If you don't want to keep it, why worry about spotting?" the doctor said. I faltered. "I mean, if you're having a miscarriage there's nothing we can do, but it sounds like that could make the decision for you."

I found her cold and felt we were wasting her time. But her coolness drew out conviction: I didn't want to miscarry. I wanted the baby. With every bit of complication in our lives, with the loss of what we'd thought the year would bring, I wanted it.

Huz did too. At home, I lay on the couch after a good cry. Rubbing my back slowly, Huz sat on the floor, patient and listening.

"Okay," I said. "We're going to do this?"

"I want to," he said. "It's up to you, but I want to."

"Okay." I smiled as I looked at Huz beaming as a father-to-be. I hoped our baby would inherit those blue eyes. Huz squeezed my hand and kissed my fingers. We had each other.

"We need to take you to the hospital," my midwife said. She was crouched beside me in our apartment bathroom, where between contractions I was sitting backwards on the toilet, resting my head on the cool porcelain tank.

"Okay."

I had a fever—a sign of infection and a signal that our "see how it goes" home birth needed to relocate.

As Huz helped me into the car, I saw autumn leaves in the gutter and the four a.m. lamplight shining on them; in a neighbour's window, the paper cut-out of a turkey. It was

Thanksgiving Sunday and we had already notified friends that we would be missing dinner.

Due dates are deceptive things. The system of counting the weeks of pregnancy from before conception occurs makes for odd math. In order to predict an end date (full-term birth), you work backwards from an ovulation date that would occur only in a regular twenty-eight-day cycle. Most menstruating folks have bodies and cycles that do not conform to that calculation. A due date is a guess, and even then, it is one date within an ideal range.

That said, my first baby was late.

The due date was September 30, and like many pregnant others, I was impatient for the next step, the reveal, and for the relief I expected my body to feel from carrying such a large baby in my own small frame.

On October 6, my water broke. Whoosh.

No TV or movie scene of this event had prepared me for the sudden, tremendous rush of fluid that flooded my clothes and the floor. I started to hop, trying not to step in it, and grabbed a nearby towel to stuff between my legs.

"Holy smokes!" I shouted to an empty house.

I waited, unsure what would happen if I moved. Moments later there was another gush. I stuffed more towels between my legs and walked bow-legged and wobbling to the phone. I called my midwife.

"Are you sure you didn't pee yourself? That wouldn't be unusual at this point with the pressure on your bladder."

"I've never peed such a large amount of fluid." We discussed the smell, colour and stickiness of what had left a wet spot on two parts of our carpet.

I felt exhilarated. Finally, the baby was coming. But I was not in labour.

If waters break pre-labour, there are different schools of thought in the obstetric and midwifery models, but both agree on the risk of infection. Once waters break (or the not-as-fun-as-it-sounds PROM—premature rupture of membranes—happens), there should be no bath or intercourse or anything that increases the risk of bacteria reaching the uterus now that the protective barrier is gone. In the midwifery model, a reasonable time span to wait before inducing labour was two days. My midwife let me know that the obstetric model would wait either twenty-four hours or not at all to induce.

We decided to wait.

The next day I went for as long a walk as possible. I bounced on a yoga ball. I stretched. I begged my body to go into labour. That evening, twenty-four hours after my waters had marbled the living room carpet, I had my first contractions.

Based on the timing of the contractions and the dilation of my cervix, our midwife advised that it would still be some time. She suggested we try and get some sleep. She, too, would sleep in the meantime, and she offered to do so in our guest room if I felt safer with her close by. I did.

I tried to sleep. I dozed between contractions, feeling alone with them as Huz also tried to sleep next to me. One of the photos we have from that night—out of focus in the low light of a bedside lamp—is of me sitting on the edge of the bed, my head rolling back, my hands pushing down on the mattress on either side of me, Huz kneeling at my feet with his hands on my belly as I rode through one of those early contractions. The photo sums up what I recall of those overnight hours of early labour: pain, in a blur.

My doula arrived and stayed awake with me. She had given birth for the first time less than two years before, and her reassurances echoed the memories she had of her labour: "I know it feels like it's going to come out of your bum, but I promise you it won't." We laughed. It was hard to tell with the incredible abdominal pressure what was pushing where.

But I was fighting a fever, and eight hours into what would be a twenty-hour labour, I needed the support of a hospital birth.

I have since learned that on weekends and holidays, in hospitals, you hold your breath and wait for the time to pass, fingers and toes crossed for no emergencies in the span that doctors are on call or being covered for. Operations run less smoothly than on weekdays and never according to plan. I didn't know this then, when my midwife called the hospital I was registered at and was told I had to be taken elsewhere due to short staffing. I felt nervous at things slipping away: a home birth and now the hospital I was familiar with. But the contractions quickly distracted me.

"Noooooooooo!" I bellowed from all fours on the floor in the back seat of our minivan. It was the only position that made having contractions in transit palatable. At the doors of Emergency, I was helped into a wheelchair, and my doula dug out elastic bands to pull my hair off my sweating face. (Later, when I saw the photos from this day, my vanity frowned: *my hair was in pigtails the whole time?*)

In the delivery ward, I climbed in and out of the bathtub, trying to find relief from pain and to cool my fever. I was angry that my midwife wouldn't permit the comfort of a hot bath, but my temperature was high, and we were trying to avoid starting antibiotics.

Later, these became part of a list of "little things": Changing hospitals. Evading antibiotics.

I bit hard on the tube of laughing gas, mostly grateful for the outlet of gripping with my teeth. I squeezed Huz's hand so hard it hurt him. I refused to put any clothes on—the sensation of clothing seemed incongruous with that of bursting open.

When it came time to push, I struggled. Pushing through contractions, I had been informed, is a skill not immediately available to all. I felt inept and confused. I pushed. I bit. I squeezed. I screamed. It had been hours of incredible pain.

The baby was crowning, finally. My midwife held a mirror so that I could see the top of its head, a bit of its dark hair, inspiration to push the baby past my pelvis. But it was stuck. And meconium had been dripping out past the baby: a sign of distress. We needed help.

The overhead lights were flipped on, and the room filled with people. The obstetrician and his resident, whom my midwife deferred to, marched in with a trail of nurses behind them. Pediatricians were at the ready should the baby need assistance. The multiple players in a now-complicated hospital scene had taken their places.

"Okay, we're going to use forceps to pull baby out of you. We'll cut the umbilical cord—Dad, do you want to do that?"

We said no. I needed Huz to stay with me at the top of the bed.

"Okay, and then we'll place baby on your chest." Unless, the OB explained, the baby had swallowed any of the meconium and needed help breathing, in which case they'd first take baby over to be suctioned. "Then we'll bring it to your chest, okay?"

Okay.

With that plan in place and the strength and help of forceps, the baby was pulled out of me. I felt a wave of relief. The earthquake that had been shaking my body for hours subsided rapidly. The shift from being in pain and afraid was dramatic, like I had broken through the surface from underwater.

With that relief came jubilation. I was asking, "Is it a boy? Is it a girl?"

I couldn't wait to meet my little one, to begin to know them. The baby was not being put on my chest. I registered that events had taken that turn. I looked at the clock on the wall at the foot of the bed, and my mind did a quick ordering of numbers: our child was born at the fourth hour on the eighth afternoon of the tenth month in the sixth year of the two-hundredth decade.

I logged the series of even numbers in my thoughts. That kind of data collection was a practice I'd developed in the years in hospital rooms as a kid undergoing chemotherapy: count the tiles, count the number of red cars that go past in one hour compared to the number that go by in the next. Arrange the time of day in order from smallest to largest number. Add and identify the numbers—prime? Divisible by what?

The exercise both passed the time and was a way for me to describe the experience.

Two, four, six, eight, ten ... my baby's birth.

My mother was taking photos. She'd arrived in Vancouver from her home in California on a date we'd thought would be after the baby's birth, so she could be in town to meet and help with her first grandbaby. I hadn't expected her to be at the birth, but now that she was, we tasked her with taking pictures. One picture she captured was of the doctor who did the delivery, the resident. It is seconds after the birth, and in the photograph, you can see that the doctor is running across the room. You can see in her hands the limp body of a baby whose head is drooped to the side.

Over the years, I have looked at these photos every October 8, sometimes making it through only a few before I put them away—which is to say, I close the folder on my computer, one of the handful of places the digital images are saved. (My computer, an external hard drive, a cloud drive somewhere. I am terrified of losing them, despite how seldom I can revisit the story they tell.)

One Christmas, eight years after that day, I was with my dear friends Christine and Jean-Guy, and their son and his partner, who was pregnant. We were looking at family photos: the son as a baby thirty years earlier and his birth. Christine talked about the day, her labour, and we admired the round shape of her pregnant belly and the perfect babyness of her son after he was born. Birth stories are powerful, and most parents, I think, are moved to share them—their beauty and their challenges.

I wanted to respond in kind, to share my photos of giving birth and be a mother in that moment. My photos make many people uncomfortable. The photos and my story, for some, make their fears come true. "Your experience is a parent's worst nightmare," I've been told. It's an isolating statement, and I've wondered if they're asking me to stay silent.

But these friends are like family. I asked Christine if I could show her the photos. Just her. I trusted her capacity to be with hard stories when they are true stories. I opened my laptop and clicked through the images, describing each one. I sobbed and talked and cried and shared. I looked at every photo with her, and that was the first time I'd made it through the entire collection.

In that photo of the doctor running across the room with a limp baby in her hands, you can see me in the background, supine on the bed, as I was asking, "Is it a boy? Is it a girl?" As I looked to various faces for an answer, I discerned that the expressions were solemn. My doula's eyes were full of tears. My sense of relief was replaced with confusion and dread as I determined that all eyes were on the team working to suction meconium from my baby's lungs. No one returned my gaze.

"Glued shut" is how they would describe those lungs to us later in conversation. A conversation that referenced fetal distress, explained ischemia (a restriction of blood supply, a shortage of oxygen to tissues) and cited systemic failure. A conversation that was one of a series—meetings with our midwife, meetings with the head of obstetrics. Reports. Phone calls. Eventually a letter of complaint to the BC College of Midwives. A need to understand what had happened and a growing anger at the "little things" that could have been prevented or responded to differently, more carefully.

The admitting nurse had felt pressured by our midwife. The unit nurses said communication had been poor. The obstetrician said as soon as he walked into the room, he could smell the infection that our baby's reserves were devoted to fighting. Our midwife countered defensively that she would not have been able to smell the infection, having been in the room for hours. My fever had gone down, and so I wasn't treated with antibiotics, but upon reflection, well ... The midwifery model didn't, at that time in BC, require constant fetal monitoring in the presence of meconium, a measure that would better have anticipated the level of distress.

We listened to the list of "little things" like watching a game of hot potato.

"Each little thing on its own was not an issue. In retrospect, we can see how they added up."

"Sometimes, babies just die."

In fact, in Canada, about one in three hundred births ends in "neo-natal death," the death of a baby soon before, during or after birth. Following the path of responsibility for these deaths is circuitous, without a clear end.

"What if" is one of the most painful questions humans can ask themselves. What if I'd been induced? What if we had gone to the hospital we were registered at? What if we had chosen a different midwife? What if I had done any one little thing differently? Could everything that followed have been changed?

I wrote:

All the trouble you've seen, all the pain that you have
Could have it been prevented? You ask

It's a question that keeps you from sleeping
It's a story that you always replay
And you watch for that pivotal moment
When everything changed
It leaves a bad taste in your mouth
You try and try but it won't come out
It casts a shadow of a doubt
It weighs heavy on your chest
But for the weary there is no rest
And you only did your best

"You made the best decisions based on the information you had," my therapist would remind me for years as I struggled with regret and responsibility and shame and anger. Did I? I sometimes still need to remind myself of her words. I sometimes still ask, *what if?*

On that day in the delivery room, as worry swelled, I turned my head to Huz. We kept our eyes and hands locked together. For ten minutes, the doctors urged our baby's survival.

The obstetrician approached us and began, "I'm so sorry, but your baby has died—" Huz cried out, and I froze, but before the doctor's words could fully land on our shoulders, a shout from across the room commanded, "Wait!"

The team had convinced a heartbeat to return in our baby's body. The doctor retracted his statement, telling us hurriedly that they would keep trying, and the team whisked our son from the room to continue the work of resuscitation.

Our son.

A nurse approached us and asked his name. We had lists of names. We had imagined that we would have hours and days to spend with our new baby, trying each name on for size. In that moment, I struggled to recall any name on any list. Huz and I looked at each other, he too forgetting, and we simultaneously asked out loud, "Emmett?" Our question in unison answering itself.

Two *E*s, two *M*s, two *T*s. Emmett.

An hour later, we were able to see him. He was intubated through his mouth and had multiple access lines placed in his arms. He was still covered in vernix and blood. I stared. My midwife said, "It's okay for you to touch him," and I brought my hand to his head, being careful of cuts on his forehead that the forceps had made.

"He was bigger than we anticipated," the doctor said, to explain those cuts. I marvelled at Emmett's size—over ten pounds. I withdrew my hand, feeling unsure and disconnected. I didn't know where to touch him. I wanted to pick him up and pull him toward me. To leave that room with him safe in my arms. At the same time, I wanted to shut my eyes and escape alone. I was overwhelmed.

Emmett was transferred to BC Children's Hospital; Huz went with him. I was wheeled back to my room, where I would wait six shocked and silent hours until there was a team available to transfer me too. As I was being helped into bed, my midwife shared that years earlier, she had lost a child in a premature delivery.

I stared at her and thought, *Why are you telling me this unrelated story? My baby is fine. They are taking him to the other hospital, where he will be fine.* Instead I expressed some kind of sympathy. I imagine she was wanting to relate, or was herself overcome with reminders, I don't know. In the moment, perhaps it was clear to everyone around me that Emmett was unlikely to survive, and they were ready to say so out loud. But I could not believe in an outcome other than his survival and wanted no other information.

Alone in the delivery room, the midwife gone to complete paperwork, my doula and mom having stepped away for food and phone calls, someone helped me into clean hospital gowns. I wished I could fall asleep, exhausted from the hours of labour and wanting out of the intense unknown. My mother's husband had arrived from California; he sat in the room quietly with me, and later I wished I'd asked him to hold my hand.

Huz was in shock and alone across the city, waiting while Emmett underwent tests to determine the extent of the injury of his birth. This was before cell phones were common, and I tried to make a phone call from my room to the nurse's station to reach Huz, to get any kind of update. I knew nothing of what was going on. In my thoughts, I heard noise and silence, both in extremes.

Meanwhile, other phone calls had reached family, who began to make their way to the hospital waiting rooms. Huz's parents boarded an airplane toward us.

The paramedics who transported me between hospitals kept referring to me as "Mama." I blinked at them, disbelieving. They were cracking jokes and seemed cavalier on the job, a veneer I would learn in the coming years to be common among paramedics. But they hushed when they wheeled my stretcher into the Neonatal Intensive Care Unit, into the one private room there.

Another photo I have from that day: me still on the stretcher, pulled up next to Emmett's infant bed adorned with blinking machinery and strung with IV tubing, my hand reaching out to hold his. He is still intubated through the mouth and unconscious, and his head is turned to me. My face is crumpled.

"Take it easy there, Mama," the paramedics said as they helped me down off the stretcher.

The nurses carefully moved Emmett and all his medical extensions into my arms for the first time. Huz added his arms around us. It was near midnight, and as three we held on to each other, reunited in grief, in love and in awe.

The photos taken then are tender and heartbreaking, our gentle touch discovering Emmett's face and limbs. Huz's head in his hands. Tears endless on my cheeks. Love; grief; love; grief.

"Try and get some sleep," the nurses said. Not technically discharged myself, I had been transferred to the attached Women's Hospital, where I lay down in the hospital bed and Huz lay on a cot beside me. We must have slept. And somehow, we woke.

We met with the doctors that morning.

"Emmett will not speak, or move, or open his eyes; he will have no internal life," they said.

They explained that if extubated now, Emmett would die, likely quickly, as his body was showing no reflex to fight back; his body was not trying to breathe on its own. But if we did not extubate soon, his body might recover strength and begin to breathe on its own. And then we would have a breathing body, but no brain activity.

"A vegetable," they said. And I thought, *but he's my vegetable and I will hold him and care for him. Get out of my way.* We asked for time; it was still morning.

It mattered to Huz and his family that Emmett be baptised. The hospital chaplain was called, a suitably gentle man professionally skilled at adapting to the immediate beliefs and desires of families. He performed the ceremony in the now-crowded NICU room. Huz chose Emmett's middle name: Christopher. The patron saint of travellers.

The chaplain gave us a candle that I still light annually on the anniversary of this day. I'm careful not to burn it for long; I need it to last.

Come afternoon, I begged time to slow down, my wont to look at the clock and calculate permutations not serving me well—I only added up the evidence of time slipping away. The question of whether Emmett's body would live or not became theoretical—we had no choice but to let him die, as his body was deteriorating. The choice we could make was when. I stalled.

Cousins and friends arrived at the hospital to meet him. In later months, in moments of grief and disbelief, I would recite the names of the people who came. Anita. Colin. Paris. Eric. Philippa. They were proof that Emmett existed; they were people who could assure me, "Yes, he was here. We saw."

Come evening, we left the NICU and were taken into a room nearby with low light and stiff couches. With Emmett in our arms, the doctor and nurse extubated him and left the room swiftly, closing the door carefully behind them.

We spoke. We waited. His death was quick and imperceptible. No movement, no sound.

There are a few blurry photos that we took in this room. I'm reminded of the era of portraits that the living would take with a dead family member. In the 1800s, when people had to sit very still for the long exposure times of cameras, the deceased family member would be the only one completely in focus, as no breath had moved their body during the time the photo was taken.

In children's hospitals, especially with babies who die in utero or soon after birth, families can choose to spend time dressing their baby and taking photos if they desire. Some dress them in clothes they had chosen for their baby. I felt alarmed at the thought of Emmett being handled. When I was asked if I'd like to keep a trimming from his hair, I had a strong reaction. No; his body should remain intact, sacred. I wanted to be as still as he was. I wanted to die with him.

After a time, we invited family members into the room to hold his body, and after that we called a nurse to take his body away; she did so, tenderly, from my arms into hers and out of the room. These memories are painful and foggy. No matter how many times I've tried to look more closely at them, I can't glean any further details.

For months, the motion of extending my arms—the motion of giving his body to the nurse—was one I found hard to repeat, no matter what I was holding. The body memory too strong to remind me of anything other than letting go of him. I would reach to accept a glass of water and feel an instant twinge.

We went home that night, and I waited outside in the courtyard while Huz disassembled the crib we had arranged in our bedroom. I wouldn't enter until he had. The crib was moved into the spare room with all the other baby items we had collected; a room to which the door remained closed for months. A room that eventually would be sorted through, some items put into labelled boxes and stacked in a closet, others given away. A desk and a guest bed moved in, though not for years.

Once the crib was apart, I tiptoed indoors and looked around. Our home seemed unfamiliar, now—he should be here. I sat at our dining table while people puttered in our kitchen—our mothers or friends, I'm not sure. Their presence felt meaningless, though it must have been useful in some practical ways. I don't know how long they stayed. I don't know when we fell asleep.

At the table I picked up a pen and wrote our son's name on the back of a piece of mail waiting to be opened. I had during pregnancy scribbled so many names on paper while we brainstormed, naming being one of my favorite acts of anticipation.

Emmett Christopher. Two *E*s, two *M*s, two *T*s; a traveller.

CHAPTER 6 EVERY WALTZ I CAN THINK OF

On the one-year anniversary of Emmett's death, Huz and I returned for the first time to Lighthouse Park—the place we'd gone the same day I decided to carry my pregnancy, when I first knew I wanted Emmett. Through the brush and over the rocky hillside, we pushed, climbed and reached a plateau of stone to sit on and look at the grey sea. The wind smacked our red cheeks and we gripped each other's hands.

"What do we do now?" I said of Emmett's death, of the anniversary, of the paths before us. Autumn would soon settle into West Coast winter, the second time we'd face the long, wet season on the other side of losing a child. I was going to make my second album, that I knew. If I wasn't going to be a mother, I was going to try to resume the career I had been so excited about. I could only partly remember eagerness, and going back to music seemed like a distant second choice. But I was drawn to it, still. Huz was going to apply to grad school. He too was dusting off the memory of previous goals and ambitions, rebuilding ideas of the future.

We talked about our cautious steps forward, and even more carefully imagined what our lives would hold beyond the next year. Another album, an MFA: what else did we want?

Huz was nervous, I could tell. He was mumbling and looking away. "I have a present for you, but I'm not sure if it's good timing or not," he said, half asking if it was, half apologizing in advance if it wasn't.

He reached into his pocket and pulled out a silver box. Without words, I told him to open it for me. He did, and inside, a diamond ring. My first thought: *How much money did you spend on this?* We didn't have much. He knew what I was thinking.

"It was my grandmother's!" he said. She had died the summer before, not long before Emmett. Huz told me about having gone with his mother and her family to sort through his grandmother's things. When it came to her engagement ring, Huz spoke up. "Can I have it?" His mother, aunts and uncle had paused to understand the request and then cheered, realizing his hope and intention.

"Oh!" I said. I was moved by the family connection, and by all of them keeping that moment a secret for over a year.

"I know this day will always be incredibly sad," said Huz. "But I want to add some happiness to today. And he brought us here."

We had talked about getting married before. Despite myself, I had said I wanted a proposal. This was after years of insisting I didn't want to get married at all, partly waiting until same-sex marriage was legal in Canada (the Civil Marriage Act had been recognized two years prior), and partly wanting to resist the norm. I didn't want to admit my attraction to the ritual—the dress, the party, the speeches.

I wondered if I could be a good feminist, much less a good queer, if I married a cis man. All of that went out the window with my being in love with Huz. I adored him. And we were tied by the experience of losing our son; that tie took precedence. We'd also been carried through this loss by our family and community. I imagined a wedding that would honour them, a chance to celebrate and thank those who had cared for us.

"Will you marry me?"

Yes.

We took pictures of our crying eyes, of our hands together and a ring that glimmered like the sea behind it. We look windswept and oblivious to the cold in every shot. We were sure the worst was behind us, and we started to dream of what was ahead. I got out a notebook while we were sitting on the rock in Lighthouse Park, jotting down questions I already had about wedding plans, more ready to throw a party than either of us had realized. The quickness of my shift into planning mode unsettled Huz, though he didn't tell me that until months later.

A date. A venue. A cake. A caterer. A dress. Plus countless handmade and vintage items that I revelled in making and collecting. I wrapped the reception like a gift for each person there. We didn't want a DJ or a cover band. Instead our favourite local band, C.R. Avery and the BoomChasers, performed. We sang along and cheered; all our family and friends danced around us. The night was conviviality at its finest.

Not meaning to, I got pregnant again, on our late-summer honeymoon. I'd just come back from my second album's first tour. Huz wasn't halfway through the first semester of his MFA. The thud of an unexpected pause in my career with another unplanned pregnancy passed quickly: I wouldn't lose the chance to have a child again, even if I hadn't planned to. This time, I wanted the baby from the start. I hoped, and I wrote:

Will you stay this time?
Your sway with the gods will be stronger than mine
Tell them, hey, your mama needs a break
Make them let you stay

———

Because our first child had died, my pregnancy was closely monitored. Emmett's death had been circumstantial, but it revealed secrets of both nature and Western medicine to us—all the cracks you can slip through, all the turns that can set you off course. I was being followed by Dr. G, an OB/GYN I'd met during my pregnancy with Emmett and the doctor who performed two surgeries on me after his birth to repair damage my body had sustained. I trusted her. She had tight curls, colourful glasses and wide hips and was fast during appointments, but attentive. She was brilliant and the expert to see when we realized I would need surgery. She once mentioned she had heard me on the radio.

"Did you say, 'I know her vagina'?" I joked.

"I said, 'I know *her*,'" she replied with an eye-roll.

At twenty weeks, I went for a routine ultrasound. Huz was with me. The ultrasound technician showed us the baby's face, arms, legs.

"Do you want to know the sex?"

Yes.

When I was pregnant with Emmett, I had wanted to delay that knowledge until the birth. I wanted my baby to be left alone from the projections of gender for as long as possible. But when Emmett died at a day old, I wished I had had longer with the fantasy of who he was, even if it was just a fantasy. I decided in this pregnancy that I wanted as much information as possible to paint a picture of who this little person might be.

"It's a boy."

Another son. Brothers. I exhaled into imagining this story of their lives.

The technician continued to probe and prod. I desperately needed to pee. It was taking a long time. She seemed distracted, and when she stepped out of the room, I said to Huz that perhaps she was new to the job. She came back. More prodding and imaging. She seemed confused. She left to show the images to a doctor and asked us to wait. Only a faint dot of worry had dropped on my mind before we were led out of the dark room.

"We have some concerns about the heart."

Everything slowed. As the doctor spoke, I couldn't look at Huz, but I sensed his body stiffen with fear. Mine did too. I couldn't bear what we were hearing or his worry beside me.

We were to speak to Dr. G as soon as possible, they said. She would go over the results and next steps with us.

It was January, and Vancouver had been struck by an uncharacteristic and crippling snowfall over Christmas. Vancouver is a city that halts under snow, and these few weeks after the holidays, snow still lined the streets. Having returned to work and life after the initial upset, people still unhappily manoeuvred through it.

I stood on the passenger side of the car and couldn't see how I'd gotten out of the car and over the small curbside snow-mountain in front of me, much less how I'd get back in. The drive home was like pushing through a noisy crowd; we spoke little but the traffic clamoured around us.

Back at our apartment, we turned the phone off and lay in the dark; less sensory input simplified the heaviness of *something is wrong*. But we didn't turn the phone back on in time and missed the call from Dr. G. We watched TV to numb out and pass the time; we went to bed anxious.

She reached me the next day at work, and I took the call away from my desk, in the quiet of an empty office.

"Of all the people this could happen to, I am so sorry this is happening to you," she said.

I was crying and terrified. "Is he going to be okay?"

"I don't know. It is serious."

A full day of tests and meetings was scheduled at BC Women's Hospital. First, a detailed fetal echo performed by a cardiologist to image the baby's heart. It was in that room that we were told: hypoplastic left heart syndrome. It is rare, we were told. It is very serious. There are options.

We moved from one waiting room to another, holding but not drinking bad coffee, shifting between carrying hot paper cups at the rim and cradling their shape as the liquid cooled. In a small meeting room, we sat at a round, low table with a group of cardiologists, geneticists and a nurse practitioner, and the information continued: There is no known cause. It affects approximately one in four thousand babies. There is no cure, but HLHS babies can survive.

Huz and I sat close together but made little physical contact, out of stress. We were asked to consider:

Termination (though largely unsupported, due to the number of life-saving interventions available for HLHS and a 70 per cent rate of children reaching adulthood). I answered before they continued—no. I couldn't. The baby was already kicking and moving, and I couldn't bear to choose to end his life. I'd already had an abortion. I'd already lost a child at full term. I couldn't. I shot a look at Huz and tried to gauge whether he could terminate, not because that would sway me, but because I hoped it wasn't something we would fight about. He shrugged, agreeing and feeling helpless.

Okay, they said. Then:

Compassionate care: to carry the baby to term but to allow his heart—and him—to die, as they would in the outside world without intervention, usually in one to two weeks after birth. I felt so afraid of any experience like the one we had already had. To give birth and hold that baby until death was an agony I knew. Here, I didn't look at Huz. I was starting to tremble.

Thus:

The modification route, in which a series of three surgeries (at birth, roughly six months and four to five years old) modify an HLHS heart to function adequately.

Or:

Organ transplant, joining the wait-list at birth.

Huz nodded, trying to take in the bombardment of information. I felt nearly conquered by it and hoped he would remember details I was losing track of. We were reeling, stunned and fighting to think clearly.

Over the next few weeks, we researched and consulted, spoke to more nurses and doctors, read online forums. I felt frozen by the options, by their consequence and importance. We chose.

We travelled to Edmonton to pursue the modification route. There were no surgeons in BC at the time who could perform the surgery the baby would require at birth, so we were transferred to the Stollery Children's Hospital, whose halls I knew intimately from the months I had spent there when I was a kid with cancer.

My own care had already been transferred from beloved Dr. G to a team of perinatologists. "I wish I didn't have to let you go and that I could take care of you to the end," she'd said, sitting on the round stool at our last appointment together, pulling off gloves as she spoke but not breaking eye contact.

Me too.

Sometime earlier, I had named the baby Thomas Kihew. I hadn't dreamed the name, exactly, but it appeared in my mind, like it had always been there. He was born by scheduled c-section, all the players in his care ready and waiting to take the stage. I held him close to my chest for half an hour after his birth. I studied what I could of his over-nine-pound body—big and new.

"I don't know who Thomas Kihew is, but you don't look like him," I told this baby. "I love you, I love you, I love you," I said as the transport nurse took him in her arms to move him from the delivery room to the critical care unit in an incubator-type box. (Months later, we would show him a picture of himself in this moment: "Look! Your spaceship!")

My body remembered what it was to give birth to Emmett and not get to hold him. I had to assure myself over and over that this would be different. That my distance from this baby was temporary.

We called him Baby Boy for the next few days.

"What about Ford?" Huz asked.

"Like the verb?"

"Like the writer."

At first I couldn't picture it, but the name felt increasingly right, like growing daylight revealing a landscape. The name seemed strong, and it suited this little bundle who had come into the world having to fight. Ford's first open-heart surgery took place when he was nine days old. His second, at four months.

I can't describe these months now—their intensity, their stress, their fear, their hope, their slow passing. The memories hurt too much still. It may be that they will stay without words forever.

I *can* tell you there were also moments of joy, of gazing into and getting to know our little one's blue eyes, of smiling and playing. We were transferred back to the hospital in Vancouver, where breaks on the rooftop patio and the surrounding lawn punctuated our new normal with what we'd imagined life with a new baby would be. We developed a routine of one of us always being at the hospital with Ford while the other went home to sleep, shower, eat toast made from bread found in the back of the freezer, pause. I was on mat leave, and Huz had planned to take the summer off before he started his MFA again in the fall. We were rarely at home at the same time, Huz and I, but we found time to be together as a new family at the hospital. We got to know nurses like familiar faces in the neighbourhood.

At six months, the modification route was not serving Ford properly, and the "T word" returned to the table.

HLHS kids who have modification treatment are likely to need a heart transplant by the time they reach twenty. Ford needed a replacement heart much sooner than we had imagined.

The options we'd been given during the pregnancy were slipping away quickly. To be listed for a transplant, we were moved again—this time to SickKids hospital in Toronto.

We had only a couple days to make the move, to find a house (and cat) sitter for our home in Vancouver, to pack, again, for an unknown length of time, to notify friends, and to meet with the social worker to apply for funding to get us to Toronto and secure us a place to stay. The moves always happened in a hurry. Each transfer involved a private jet for Ford with one of us, his parents, accompanied by two paramedics and one cardiologist. The other parent would fly domestic. The paramedics would tend to Ford, who travelled in a transport incubator, and both times I joined the flight, I was strapped to a gurney—there wasn't much room for non-medical passengers on board. Ford was generally a relaxed passenger, but on the way to Toronto, he started to kick and cry. I could hear the paramedic trying to settle him, checking his oxygen and his meds, but not finding the solution. I craned my neck and suggested, "Check his diaper." Ford, who tolerated breathing and feeding tubes in his nose, IVs in his arms, had not an ounce of patience for a poopy bum.

The paramedic chuckled. "I hadn't thought of that!" I returned to the view from my reclined position at the back, glad at least to be able to mother from a distance.

—◆—

In Canada, most organ transplants come from the States. We just don't have the population here, but we benefit from being close to a country with a large population—HLHS babies in an isolated place like Australia rarely list for or receive a transplant. There is a higher number of organ transplants done around American long weekends too—accidents, drunk driving. For those on a transplant list, long weekends in the US inspire a kind of tense waiting.

But a transplant is a complicated thing to hope for. I found that I couldn't, not exactly. I wanted my son to live, but I could never wish for someone else's child to die. We had already watched our son Emmett die—I could not hope for that suffering in another family.

"You're not hoping someone dies. You're just hoping that if, God forbid, something happens to a child, the parents choose to donate the organs," a nurse rationalized.

So I hoped for that choice and not for the events that would have to lead to it, uncertain in my conscience of the distinction.

I questioned my motherhood: Should I wish for my son's life at all costs? The cost of another's life? The quality of his own, if the wait went on too long?

—◆—

The heart heard through ultrasound makes a "whoosh whoosh" washing machine sound, and I have always liked that sound of the muscle pumping fluid. I remember learning that the heart beats in 3/4 time, a waltz.

One day, during the long wait for someone else's heart, I was singing "Rainbow Connection" to Ford at his bedside. Next to the twice-made sternotomy scar, I tapped the rhythm lightly on his chest, 1-2-3, 1-2-3. I sang every waltz I could think of to Ford and his heart. When I ran out, I made up new ones. 1-2-3, 1-2-3, *please stay, please live*, 1-2-3, 1-2-3. My complicated prayer for his survival danced daily. Ford responded with wide eyes and smiles, holding our gaze and laughing, happily sucking on a soother, flipping pages of board books, watching the birds on the mobile above his head endlessly circle, always amazed that they kept coming back. The waiting was a torment, living in the fishbowl of a hospital room a strain; being with him was a joy.

You're not supposed to know where a donor heart comes from, but a nurse let "New York" slip. Since we were waiting in Toronto, we were comforted by her blunder that at least the heart would have a short flight.

That morning, a phone call had woken us from sleep.

We had an apartment in Midtown owned and furnished by the Ronald McDonald House and made available to "long-term" families like ours rather than a room in the shared house. We'd been waiting in the city five months already; Ford had just turned one.

"There's a potential donor; you should come in straightaway."

Our own hearts racing, we dressed and pushed ourselves out of the building and onto the subway. The surgeons could be leaving to harvest the heart within hours. Harvest: to reap and collect. A word I'd always associated with bounty and nature, not a body dismantled in an operating room.

We spent the morning nervous, excited at Ford's bedside, texting family members, "We think it's happening."

The surgeon who came in to give us an update joked this would be their first-ever daytime transplant, telling us that transplants had a way of taking place overnight. More updates came in every few hours and it turned out that overnight would still be the case, as the remarkable choreography between hospitals across North America unfolded: the donor baby, the family's choice, was providing multiple organs that day, and the removal of the heart was the last move. Our doctors had to wait for the other teams' dance to be completed before they could take this final step.

Later, I wrote this song:

On the night of your death
They scattered your breath
Across the continent
You know there's a list
Waiting for accidents
Just like this to happen
And when your heart arrived on its private jet
You know this momma cried for the life it left
And now it's buried here

I ached for the family whose child died that day. I concentrated hard, facing south, breathing, "I'm so sorry, I'm so sorry, your baby, I'm so sorry ..." and "thank you, thank you, thank you." I was wordless with wonder.

Despite the months of waiting for that day, that hour, it seemed sudden as Ford was wheeled into the operating room for a heart transplant. Friends came to the hospital to wait with us. We had pizza and played board games in the empty cafeteria, aware of and not needing to name the tension, collectively pushing through time when it felt brutally slow and thick.

After midnight, they left to sleep and hope at their homes. We found couches in a dark waiting room (darkness to rest in is coveted in the perpetual light of hospitals) and tried to do the same. I could have sworn I didn't fall asleep, yet I was woken by the surgeon's voice searching, "Ford's parents?"

Our son had survived. I felt a crashing relief and an urgency to see him.

We thanked the surgeon, though he seemed to shrug it off. Where can gratitude go for a heart transplant? The family who donated. The pilot of the plane. The nurses in the OR. The system designed for these procedures. The years of research and development. The surgeon was doing his job, playing his part in a complex web of time and events and luck, but it was hard not to credit his trained hands for the life-saving work.

We waited and waited again. We called the nurse's station and were told to keep waiting, that the nurses were still getting him settled. And then we saw him, our Ford, miraculously on the other side of a mind-boggling procedure. Our Ford at the beginning of another stage of hyper vigilance— watching for any sign of rejection, beginning the work of balancing immune suppressants for his body to accept the foreign organ.

That night, twenty-four hours after the start of the transplant surgery, Huz left the hospital to sleep at the apartment. There was an available room on the ward upstairs—you can't sleep in the ICU if you're not a patient, except slumped in a chair at the bedside. For every night Ford spent there, we had slept apart from him. But while he was still in this critical post-op condition, we wanted one of us to be in the hospital.

There are budget and billing concerns when you're trying to find a place to sleep in the hospital. Since Ford was a patient of the ICU, I took bedding from his unit up to the ward, so that my use of their resources would be negligible. They were doing us a favour. The nurse assured me, "I will phone you if there is the slightest concern."

Upstairs I fell into a deep, exhausted sleep. I woke with a start and looked straight to the clock—it was almost nine a.m. My first thought: How could I have slept for so long? My second: But the phone didn't ring. He's okay. The phone didn't ring.

I returned to the ICU and found Ford, on day two of his life with his new heart, stable and steady and continuing to recover and improve. The hope I had was an entirely new sensation. I could imagine our long hospital stay coming to an end; I allowed myself to picture us going home to Vancouver together.

—◆—

I used to know the anatomy of the human heart. I could draw a map complete with names, reiterating lines of the blood flow—into the heart, into the lungs, out of the heart—and I did so, often. The map grew simpler over time: I learned to draw it as four squares with straight lines showing what went where.

I memorized those lines to understand the workings of Ford's uncommon heart. I learned to draw the shortened journey of blood and its detour of the lungs, the blue blood in and out, the small aorta. I can no longer easily recall the language of ventricle and atrium. I *can* remember the weight of a human heart in my hand—Ford's.

After he received the transplant, we asked to see our son's "old" heart. I thought of it as his birth heart, the new one beating within him "adopted." We were apparently the first parents to make such a request. The request was met with hesitation by the doctors but eventually, "I don't see why not." They were curious about our curiosity.

After months of going up in the hospital elevator , Huz and I were led down—down a floor, down one hall and then another. Toronto's SickKids hospital is composed of buildings new and old, stitched together by halls that shift from having bigger windows to smaller ones.

We were seated next to each other at a large table in a fluorescent-lit room, one that seemed more suited for board meetings than the handling of organs, and given plastic gloves to wear.

What did the heart arrive in? A velvet box? An unmarked Tupperware container? My nervousness obscured the presentation. But—

Huz held it first and I peered, wide-eyed and reluctant. We were being watched by the doctors, and I wished we could have been alone for a moment of reverence. We carefully turned Ford's birth heart in our hands and saw where it was scarred from multiple surgeries. We could see where the changes had been made, changes that implored his HLHS heart to adapt: the Norwood procedure, the Glenn procedure, the shunt.

For these, I would continually draw and erase lines on the heart map.

Ford's "old" heart in our hands following the transplant was brown and cold and rubbery. The doctors reminded us that it was dead tissue now. I had to laugh and admit that I'd expected something still red and throbbing.

The pathologist seemed thrilled to walk us through this part of his job and embarked on a comprehensive anatomy lesson. I wanted to be less frightened than I was; I wanted to be scientific. But the stillness of his birth heart, a heart that had also beaten within me, was an eerie reminder of death. I didn't want to touch it any longer. I was anxious to return to our son, to wind out of these halls and back upstairs.

"He's pink!" was all I could say when we first saw him after the transplant.

HLHS babies are always blue babies—cyanosis, it's called—and every one of his features that I'd admired looked suddenly different. In a way, I didn't recognize him.

I reached for him, his newness. The swelling of his face and neck from poor circulation had diminished. Even being just out of an eight-hour surgery, he already looked a great deal healthier. Not only pink, but with a neck we hadn't seen in months, his body now circulating fluid adequately, the strong, adopted heart blindly, diligently doing its work. Twelve hours after the transplant, Ford's recovery was described by the staff as remarkable, unexpected, amazing and free of any complication—vastly different from the predictions we'd been counselled on the day before the surgery when the odds were not in Ford's favour, yet the operation was still deemed "worth trying" because it was his "only chance." Our pink baby had beat the odds. Being on the other side of the waiting period was a new lease.

—◆—

A trend in design in recent years—in jewellery, on posters and T-shirts—has been "the anatomically correct heart." I cringe at the phrase when I hear it, moving to "was my son's body incorrect?" Is mine that grew him?

Since I have a disability, I have fought against words like "normal" and "natural" regarding how my body is shaped and how it moves. "Typical," and conversely, "atypical," are the terms I prefer. This fight is that of many in defence of their bodies and minds, from weight to height to mental health.

The truth is, our insides can grow with as much difference as our outsides. There may be a blueprint for the function of our organs and internal systems, but deviation from that plan is not necessarily wrong; to perpetuate "anatomically correct" can deny the diversity of our bodies, as they develop on their own or as we may modify them during our lives.

I hold strong to the belief that placing values of better or worse on the differences in our bodies—how they appear and how they function, visibly or invisibly—is dangerous. Yet it's a fact that Ford's heart "defect" meant his body, as it developed, could not survive.

When my leg was amputated, it was the cure for the cancerous tumour growing below my knee. Without amputation, I would have died. And what is terminal cancer but rogue cells that the body or treatment cannot override? Is illness a defect?

Wearing a prosthetic leg is a simple body modification compared to replacing an organ, yet it's the assistance I use most often to physically move in the world. I also use crutches and wheelchairs at times. Without these assistive devices, I wouldn't be able to cross a room, save for hopping on one leg or doing a lopsided crawl on the floor. Unlike a person with two non-disabled legs, I will never get up from a chair and walk out the door without assistance. I love these differences. It took me time to celebrate them, but how clever of bodies to adapt and of humans to design adaptations.

In Ford's pre-transplant life, his poor circulation meant that his body grew multiple collateral veins—he had more veins than "normal"—which on x-rays showed up as new lines of light. His body needed those additional veins to increase the paths for oxygen. I loved his brilliant body for forming new passages.

Ford's life was medicalized; his body needed assistance. I hoped as a mother with a disability, I could help him normalize his own. But it would be ongoing—finding my own messy middle between health and difference, function and accessibility.

"Ford isn't perfect," I had said to a therapist when my son was about eleven months old, referring to the delays in his development that were due to his time in hospital, his surgeries, multiple strokes—his life with HLHS.

She corrected my statement, almost sternly:

"He is perfectly Ford."

The words sank in.

I wanted Ford to be safe and to be spared surgeries and pain. I would have loved that for him from the start, but that is not what happened. So I wanted him to receive the assistance he needed to do his best in this world.

I loved him as he was: not anatomically incorrect. Perfectly Ford.

The second time we were woken in the night by a phone call, it had the same urgency as the first, but very different news. It was less than a month since the transplant, and Ford was suffering a massive brain hemorrhage.

It was still dark out, three or maybe four a.m., while we waited for a cab. I hated the time it took for the cab to arrive and the time it took to drive near-empty streets. My eyes darted from landmarks to street signs, tracking the familiar route between the apartment and the hospital, pushing the worst thoughts from my mind. Huz and I didn't speak; the anxiety was too familiar and too much for words.

When we arrived, they were wheeling him into surgery. Paperwork was shoved into our hands. Every hope was crashing around us. It was the second time we had to make the decision for our child: Should he live or should he die. It was the second time of eventually having no choice. He was dying.

A doctor commented that Ford's adopted heart would be the last thing to go. After fourteen months of struggle following being born with a heart not made for this world, his heart was now his strongest part.

"I'm sorry that the heart's family thinks it lives on," I said, thinking of the donor family's choice to share their child's organs.

"They'll never know that it doesn't."

I wanted to tell them.

At Ford's memorial, I asked a friend to mention his adopted heart to those gathered there. I couldn't speak, but I wanted people to know that when they visit Ford's grave, they are visiting part of that New York baby too. I wanted all of us remembered.

At a writing workshop in Banff, I read aloud a section of the above: the night of the transplant.

I had seven minutes, and the excerpt I chose didn't include that Ford had died, just that he had received a heart. I didn't think through the impact of the truncation. After the reading, several people came up to me, amazed at his survival, moved by the procedure.

"How is he now?" they asked. And I realized I had misled them.

I felt terrible for a moment, and briefly confused. To me, *of course* he died. This truth is repeated in my body and thoughts constantly. And isn't it written in my eyes? Isn't it obvious that I'm a grieving mother? Hasn't the world been so clearly changed in my son's absence?

But I looked at the awe in their eyes at the remarkable story of the little boy who survived the much-needed transplant, and I waited. I waited and felt it too: what a wonder. I waited because in their presence, he was alive again. I started to imagine the update they were looking for. He would be, what—five? Six years old now?

Yes.

I didn't want to tell them he had died; I liked their version of the story too much.

CHAPTER 7 JUST IS AND NEEDS TO BE

Vancouver had been racing toward me: I was driving west from Toronto solo, planning to make the drive in as little time as possible. Cramming twelve, thirteen, fourteen hours of driving in each day, keeping my eyes on the horizon until they burned and begged for rest.

I'd been on the road for two months, touring my third album. First the cross-Canada drive east, peppered with performances in cities across the country; then a trip to Germany, where the density of cities made for slower, easier days of touring; and then the drive home. The return held no shows, just longing for the tour to end. In Manitoba, it began to snow. By the time I reached the Alberta border, a snowstorm whipped across the prairies.

Vancouver slowed its pace, a lion crouched and ready to pounce. Come the Rocky Mountains, the city, my home, froze in its tracks as every car on the highway passed me while I inched along, white-knuckled and cautious—the only fool without snow tires. The last stretch of that drive was one I'd completed within a day countless times. This time, it stretched over two.

Bone-weary, I pulled onto our street and parked in front of our housing co-op. I grabbed as many bags as I could carry at once, deciding not to come back for the rest until the next day. I opened the door to the apartment and poked my head in before my feet. That I said nothing already made everything different; I knew he was no longer there to greet me. Huz, my husband, had left.

―◆―

Two days before, on the brink of my grindingly slow drive over the Rockies, I'd sat on a friend's couch in Calgary. We'd been close in high school and now saw each other when I needed a place to stay on tour, both caring for our friendship but knowing we'd changed, catching up on key points without getting into much depth. She was the last friend in my two months of telling everyone about the divorce in person as I drove across the country and back.

She was newly wed, three months in.

"What should we do differently?"

I looked at my friend and her partner cuddling on the couch, remembering the days of constant affection, the sweetness and certainty I had experienced with Huz. "Avoid tragedy," I said. They laughed, but it was the only advice I could give.

―◆―

Before my flight back across the Atlantic, a stranger had picked me up at the train station in Beverley, England. Her name was Lorraine, and she was a friend of the promoter; she would also be putting me up in her spare room that night. I was grateful she was chatty. She merrily described her town to me, her childhood memories of the gothic Beverly Minster, the town's impressive landmark. It was her picking me up instead of the promoter, as planned; his son was gravely ill and had been for a couple of months.

"I don't know if you know that both of my children have died, and because of that I know there's nothing I can say that can help. But I am thinking of all of you," I emailed him when he let me know plans were changing.

"Things look hopeless, but I still have hope," he had replied, and I arrived in Beverley with my heartstrings ringing with affinity for the family I knew was struggling somewhere close by. I knew those hope-filled hopeless days so well.

The bed in Lorraine's home was luxurious, and I had the best sleep of the tour, maybe the best in years. In the morning, a kind of sunshine one doesn't expect in Yorkshire filled the bedroom. I gazed out the second-floor window at the contiguous rooftops. These were days when I felt I was seeing everything for the first time, or at least anew.

—◆—

Before Beverley, London. I was performing at The Bedford, in Balham, southwest London, as part of a showcase night with a handful of other artists. The place was packed, noisy, energized. A photographer was working her way around the room for different angles of the stage, and I caught her eye. She was beautiful, and as she passed by, I smiled with unexpected confidence.

"Hello, Christa."

That she retained my name from the MC's intro, or perhaps had scanned the poster with the night's performers, was all it took to give me a thrill. We chatted about the city, her photographs. I flirted, I think. Flirting felt foreign and I was sorely out of practice. I'd been married for five years, in the relationship for eight. For the first time in a long time, potential illuminated my body and mind. The exchange was brief, and perhaps wasted on her, but I was giddy with attraction and imagination afterwards, daydreaming possibilities for the few days I had in London.

The next morning, she emailed photographs she'd taken of me. They surprised me: I didn't look as weary or uncertain as I felt. I was glad she'd captured something different and wrote later:

London, flirting
Almost forgotten how to work it
Spotlight, pictures
And when I see them
I want to be her

The photographer, it turned out, was married. I was relieved. The spark of attraction had strengthened my heartache, and fantasizing about a fling highlighted that I was far from being ready for one. I was homesick and aware that soon I'd be returning to a home I didn't recognize.

A week before that night in London, I performed with the cellist I was touring with in the back room of a small coffee shop in Kreuzberg, Berlin, small enough that we could play unplugged. Halfway through the set, I shared that it was my birthday. The cellist led the room in a round of "Happy Birthday," and after the gig, we wandered the neighbourhood of our Airbnb looking for a bar to have a birthday drink.

That night in Berlin, I turned thirty-five.

The cellist was not just any cellist. He was an ex-boyfriend I'd broken up with cruelly, and though I still hadn't forgiven myself, he had, and we became friends; being fans of each other's music and musicianship had never changed. When I woke on the day after my birthday, I got up from my bed, walked to the living room and lay down next to him. "A giant Dutch dream," a mutual friend had nicknamed the cellist when we were dating, and as I wrapped my arms around the torso of his six-foot, four-inch body and rested my head on his shoulder, he welcomed me. My shape still remembered his shape from years before. I felt enveloped and comforted. On that tour, I increasingly tried to be close to him, and we danced around a tension between us. It made for great chemistry onstage. Off, I was dangerously pushing a boundary—he was in a relationship. He also saw better what I didn't: that I was in the earliest days of an ending and in need of consolation and forgiveness. He gave me as much of both as he could. When we said goodbye, before I travelled solo to England, I wept on the train. Any separation was so quick to hurt.

—•—

A month before that, in Edmonton, Huz's sister and her partner had come to the venue I was performing at. "Hi!" they greeted me warmly, so warmly I knew no one had told them Huz and I had separated.

A brief flare of anger with his family rose up in me— they weren't always very good at sharing what was going on in their lives. Surely the end of a marriage deserved some conversation. I couldn't bear to tell them in that moment, before I was set to sing for a room full of old friends, people I'd grown up with and their parents who were "so proud!" of me.

I hid in the storage room-turned-green room, where conversations were frequently interrupted by the kitchen staff needing something from the deep freezer. I told the other musician performing that night, "My sister-in-law is here. She doesn't know her brother and I have broken up. I feel sick."

"What's the worst that can happen?" he said. "They're going to find out eventually."

Good point.

A few days before Edmonton, in the small BC mountain town of Ymir, I sat with my friend Carla. She'd become a friend during the numerous times I'd played at her venue there. Once, at a summer music festival we both attended, we walked together by a river and compared her experiences with chronic illness to mine with a disability. I loved Carla. She was smart and strong and always reading ten books at once.

"We broke up," I told her, not looking up from my drink.

"What? What happened?"

She knew Huz too; knew his artwork.

"Everything happened," I started. "Not one thing." Huz and I hurt too much; we'd been hurt too much; we'd hurt each other too much. "Seven of our eight years together have been kind of a nightmare, in terms of what's happened. We've both been so devastated as individuals we couldn't make being a couple work anymore."

That became the template for what I would say over and over, as I told friends and family across Canada one at a time.

————◆————

The tour, when it began, was going to be my first completely solo. No bandmates, no tour manager. It was also one of my longest. Huz and I decided a month before I was leaving that we would separate, which meant he'd have that time to move out. I was keeping our apartment.

"What do we do now?" he had asked our couples therapist when the final "let's end this" decision was made, after months of trying to build a new foundation on ravaged ground.

"You go home, you take your time, you try and be gentle with each other. No next step has to happen quickly."

The first night, we still slept next to each other. By the next night, our gentleness had been consumed by bitterness, defensiveness and ache. He moved into the guest room, and walking through our home felt like pushing through underbrush—tense and thick. When I knocked on the guest room door, it opened like a backdraft.

Afraid he might take out his pain by breaking things, I packed my fragile and precious items in boxes and went to stay at a friend's. Huz and I could no longer speak and only emailed terse messages as needed. Practical stuff, like when I would leave on tour and would he feed my cat.

Our couples therapist had great style; I was distracted by her shoes, her bracelets, her different sets of glasses. She was older, serious and unsmiling but exact. "Can you put on hold the question of whether you should be together or not?" she had asked at our first visit. My gut reaction: no. I didn't say it out loud. I glanced at Huz, wondering if he was having a similar response, but he stayed looking ahead, unreadable.

"We're not really going to get anywhere otherwise," the therapist said and again suggested we put the decision on hold in order to examine the relationship. Huz and I agreed, and I meant it. The "no" I had felt initially made room for a bit of hope and a lot of longing to rebuild.

"What first brought you together?"

"Community," said Huz. "Food, music, friends." At the same time, I answered, "Sex." He scoffed that I was being glib. That golden summer we met had held all those things. The following summer had held even more, when Huz had moved in with me at the housing co-op and I was third-trimester pregnant.

Huz and I had tried to shift our relationship and get to know each other in pace with the growing baby. Nearing the autumn due date, I was content knitting sweaters and felt practical shopping for a stroller. Huz put the crib together and worked extra hours house painting to save up money. We had a baby shower, and our new common community gathered around us.

After Emmett died, Huz and I clung to each other. We each wanted so badly to help the other. We were careful and kind. We cried into each other's bodies. We spent days of darkness huddled together. We watched entire seasons of serialized television to pass the early months. We made sure we were close to one another in our days and in our thoughts.

Right after Ford died, Huz and I stayed with Christine and Jean-Guy in Ottawa, delaying returning home to Vancouver. They'd come to visit Ford a few times during our time in Toronto and were a constant source of love and support. They welcomed us with solemnity and gentle distraction as needed. It was July; it was hot. We set off for a lake swim, packing a picnic and beach towels into the car. Huz carried me into the water, a necessary help as I don't have a prosthetic leg that can get wet. I've never wanted one, water being one of the few places I can move unencumbered by devices; one of the places I can't fall. The beach and the water were busy, crowded. Huz splashed me and we laughed. I wrapped my legs around his waist, and in a moment of summer's gifts, I felt happy.

"I was watching you two in the water," Christine said later. "Getting to laugh but surrounded by people who have no idea what's happened." The contrast of tragedy and life marching on, of confrontation and reprieve.

But out of the water, and soon after, Huz and I stopped holding on to each other. Through Ford's life, we had often reached for each other without response. The intensity created a frequent disconnect—we saw life-and-death decisions differently, and that was a difficult difference to overcome. We began to fight and misunderstand and judge.

So early in our relationship, the time we might have spent building a foundation of trust and acceptance and pleasure was spent, instead, in grief and grasping.

Sometime after that day at the lake, I was kneeling on all fours in the hallway of our apartment, chest heaving from a panic attack. I forced myself to remember: breathe in for four, hold for four, exhale for four ... I couldn't recall exactly what had brought me to my knees, what combination of painful memory and the present had once again pushed me over the edge. I lifted my head to look for the time on the stove clock—eight forty-five. It took a moment's concentration to determine if that was morning or evening. It was night, I realized.

I sat up on my heels and took in my surroundings. Huz was a few feet away, curled on his side on the floor, his own sobbing body either having released him to sleep or slipped him into numbness, and I remembered: we'd been talking, and then fighting, but about nothing. The kind of fight that is only two people's pain slamming together like shields. It was eight months since Ford had died. Crawling next to Huz, I lay down, not touching him, and waited until he woke, moved, remembered or forgot too.

On another blurry day, in the bedroom, I was pounding pillows against the wall and screaming. A few minutes before, I had dropped a box of noodles in the kitchen, the early steps of an attempt to make dinner, a task I could seldom tackle in those days. The sound, the new task of having to clean up, was more than I could bear. *I can't handle this.*

Huz was home, somewhere in the apartment, but I don't know that we ever spoke about what he felt then. Or what he felt a few weeks later, when I was closing the sliding closet door, it caught on a coat and I kicked the door, breaking it.

When he was in his studio one day, smashing canvases and crying out, I thought of what I had broken and wanted to break. I sat on the floor in the hallway, knowing I should keep my distance, worried but understanding too. I looked at the closed door to his studio and repeated softly, out loud: "I love you. I love you. I love you." I didn't know what else to do.

We went on like that for months more. When someone dies, so much goes with them. Slowly, we both started working and making art. Slowly, our breakdowns came less often, the distance between them concurrently building distance between us. When Emmett died, we were drawn closer together. When Ford died, we fell apart. We were climbing out of dark places as different people.

"Do you think I'm funny?" I asked one day.

"I don't think you get my sense of humour," said Huz, and it stung.

"It was a yes or no question," I said. "What do you like about being with me?"

He searched. "I like having sex," he said.

"With me specifically?"

"It could be with anyone," he said, and I felt erased.

"Do you want to celebrate our anniversary?" I asked.

"I don't know."

Our days were like that. From my home office, I would hear the front door open when he came home from work. He'd hang his coat, go to the kitchen rifling for a snack, and then go to his own workspace. If I didn't get up to greet him,

I discovered, he would never come say hello. He said he felt stressed at home if he knew I was there and that he didn't want to see me, a sad truth for us both.

Money was a stress too. After Ford's death, we had debt to contend with and little capacity mentally, much less financially, to tackle it. With the deaths of both our sons, and during Ford's life, there were so many flights purchased, hospital cafeteria meals and take-out at home, all on credit cards; there was work missed and income lost, all in a time of crisis, when "figure it out later" was a reflexive guiding principle. From the time Ford was listed for a transplant, we were enormously supported by the David Foster Foundation, which saved us from even worse debt. But money made and owed was a point of conflict for us, a repetitive, inescapable tide.

When we spent time together, even silently watching TV, we were like water splashed on hot frying pans—any comment or question or bumped elbow ricocheting, sizzling. Resentment and tension infused our interactions, apathy at best on our good days. We both needed desperately to heal, yet managed only to poke each other's wounds.

After we decided to separate, we had one more scheduled couples therapy session; Huz didn't show.

"Are you surprised?" the therapist asked me. I wasn't. I was holding a printout of an email he'd written, wanting validation that he was cruel. It would take time for me to see my failings, too.

That summer, I'd written a song about couples counselling, likening our therapist to a zookeeper and us to pacing animals.

Careful those cages aren't locked
Careful when the animals talk because they never lie
And the questions you've been asking may need no reply

"I know you're hurting," she said, "but I have a feeling you'll feel freer sooner than you think."

Huz didn't just move out when he left. He carefully extracted all his belongings, except for any gift I'd given him and anything we shared. He took nothing of me or of us with him. Huz had painted the walls of our home a handful of colours over the years we lived there. Yellows, whites, reds, blues— we changed the walls regularly, and I loved it. He painted murals of cherry blossoms, birch branches on the walls. In every room we hung pieces of his artwork, whatever was most recent.

He took his paintings, of course, when he left, and he painted every wall white while I was away. The blank, colourless walls were the most unrecognizable feature when I returned. The room that had been his studio was completely empty. What had been filled to the rafters with canvases, paints, stained glass, tools, sketches, supplies, what had been teeming with his ideas and creativity and saturated with Huz-ness—gone. Silence.

Years later, I will digitally dig for the emails Huz and I sent each other during the road trip he took so early in our relationship. I will come to one of the first and reread words on love and economics—that love cannot be described in terms of scarcity or cost, competition or greed. He wrote effusively about love's abundance—how he saw and felt love everywhere. How he was certain that love just is; that love just needs to be. I will be taken aback by remembering the sweetness of our beginning. I had gotten used to thinking of us as being in pain, used to how we left things after filing our final divorce papers, used to the one-line answers I'd crafted about why we split up. "He didn't die," I would add, letting people know that divorce was not one of life's tragedies. A relationship ended was not one failed, and our ending was our best chance at survival. The ache of divorce paled when compared to the loss of children.

That distinction would delay me feeling this: just how sad I was to lose our marriage. It would be years of grieving my sons before I could get to grieving what I lost with their father. I see us there, Huz and me golden on a summer beach, intoxicated with the discovery of each other, and my heart aches for what we couldn't prevent. I had almost forgotten that love just is and needs to be.

CHAPTER 8   SHAPE-SHIFTER

Sitting on the edge of the tub, I looked at the large, red sore on my stump—the edges of its oval shape roughed in the heat of the shower, small bumps pushed to the surface. As usual, I concealed the sore by sliding on my prosthesis, my daily shapeshifting act from three limbs to four, from crawling to walking.

"What do you call your amputated leg?" Huz asked around the time we met.

"Technically 'residual limb.'"

"That sounds like something you can't wash off."

"Also 'stump.'"

"Like you're a tree?"

"Like part of me is."

My stump is the length of my thigh, amputated just above the knee. It's small and squishy compared to the toned muscle of my much larger right leg, the strength of which comes from over twenty-five years of doing most of the work of ambulation. When I was a kid, I would make my stump's scars look like a shark: two eyes from the small, round scars made by surgical drains, a wide smile from the incision made to sever the femur. When I tense the muscles in that leg, the shark's smile turns up at the edges.

Since then, I'd come to liken all my scars to punctuation marks: the caret on my nose, the em dash on my neck, the open bracket on my throat, the asterisk on my chest, periods on my hand and knee. The shark, punctuated, becomes a colon and a closed bracket to complete my body's pair (one mustn't leave a parenthetical hanging). Still, notably, the text equivalent of a smile.

Most of these marks are small; my stump's typography is indelibly large.

For most of my life as an amputee, not many people had seen my residual-limb-tree-stump-shark turned parenthesis-smiley. For a long time, not many people knew I was an amputee at all.

Lovers often knew only once we were peeling clothes off. Sometimes earlier than that, when a hand on my left leg either went unnoticed by me or I noticed the other person register that something under their touch felt different than expected. Otherwise, we'd reach a certain point:

"I'm going to take my leg off."

"What?"

Generally, if you've got as far as pulling pants off, you don't care much if a leg is missing or not. But I remained self-conscious about my stump and would avoid letting lovers get to know its shape through sight or touch. "But you're my favourite-shaped girl," countered one lover when I lamented my asymmetry.

With the general not-taking-our-clothes-off public, the discovery often occurred on stairs, a place my ability could not be counterfeit as I had no choice but to climb or descend them one at a time.

"Did you hurt yourself?"

"No, I'm not hurt—I only have one leg."

"What?"

People see my atypical gait and often assume injury— for most of us, it's not in our experience to see a person limping and consider they're missing a limb. Few of us are accustomed enough to differences to allow for the possibility of a person not adhering to a standard.

"You should see the other guy, right?" a man across a side street shouted for me to hear. He was telling a joke, and I could tell how I was supposed to react.

"Ha! Exactly!" But I was honestly confused. It took a moment to realise he was referring to the way I walked.

I was talking to a cashier in the grocery store about having winter colds. He was recovering from one. "But I don't need to tell you about the time it takes to heal, right?"

Wearing a prosthesis can be painful; it's often painful. I either am in touch with that pain or not giving it attention. If I see video of me walking, I notice what other people notice—one step in my stride is shorter than the other, my shoulders tip back and forth, my hips swing my left leg forward. But these details, as I move, go unnoticed by me.

"Right," I say to the cashier, and as I pick up my bags and walk away, I wonder if he takes in the full-body view of me, the one that shows clearly I'm wearing a prosthesis. I wonder what he's thinking.

—◆—

The heel of my right foot is resting on the footrest bar of a stool; I let it swing forward into the space below the table. My right knee aches a little. It often aches, these days. The heel of my prosthetic left leg hangs in the air. I know this from memory and peripheral vision, not feeling. I can move my stump from side to side and rotate the femur inside the socket. Hanging from my stump, I feel my phantom limb. The feeling clashes with my vision. Eyes closed, the phantom limb strengthens.

My phantom limb is shorter than my right leg and my prosthetic leg and is perpetually bent. My phantom knee floats just off the end of my stump. A small patch on the inside of the knee tingles, and that sensation reaches down the right side of the calf to the foot. My phantom foot has the most detailed sensation—the toes, the arch, the ankle. I bring my attention to each toe—this little piggy went to market—and sense, as I have for nearly thirty years, that I'm on the verge of being able to wiggle them. I can't. They're like toes cast in cement.

This is phantom limb sensation. If I try to wiggle my phantom toes for too long, I get a punishing stab from the toes upwards: *Stop*, they say. This is phantom pain.

Phantom pain comes in sudden, agonizing pangs. In the middle of meetings, I sometimes scare people and feel embarrassed for myself when I suddenly grip the table with both hands and cry out. The only comparable pain I've experienced was being split in two: the labour and birth of my first child.

My phantom pain can burn—not sting or smoulder, but blaze like my leg is trapped in a house on fire and the rest of me can't pull it out. The pain most often feels like bones being crushed, like a steamroller slowing to a stop on top of my leg. Occasionally, I feel an ice pick hammering into the joints.

Phantom pain is brutal torture. When I experience a flare, it comes in waves for a few hours. During the convulsions I'm in anguish, but as soon as they pass, the sensation vanishes. I cannot point to any lingering pain just like I can't point to the limb that feels it.

Phantom pain is generated in the spinal cord and the brain, in the feedback of mixed signals. Phantom pain is a cruel ghost.

—◆—

"Did you grieve your leg?" my therapist asked. Good question. "I don't think so," I said.

My determination had persisted from the time my mom told me at the dining table that my leg had to be amputated. Determination to be strong, not to be scared, to live up to my dad's frequent credo: "Coutures are tough." Determination not to be vulnerable; not to be a disappointment.

My father was thrown when I phoned him with the news. I wanted to be the one to tell him. He lived in New Jersey at the time, and he answered the phone at his desk. I could easily picture him there, surrounded by windows in the back room of the house, a solarium-turned-office, piles of books and papers on every surface, an ashtray to his left, a coffee mug holding hot water to the right, his hands ever poised over or typing on the keyboard.

"The apple of my eye!" he answered, always. "My good eye at that," he continued, always.

"Dad, are you sitting down?"

He was baffled by the news—he had been shown in ceremony that I was healed from my cancer. It was a Friday, the day after my mom and I left the hospital with the news my leg had to be amputated. He spent the remainder of the day phoning all the traditional healers he knew across Canada and the States, requesting they spend the weekend in ceremony, in prayer.

The day of the surgery, with me already changed into a gown and being transported from room to room on a stretcher, my mom, on my father's behalf, urged the surgeons to retake the x-rays.

"But we did a biopsy last week. Nothing could have changed."

"Her father believes that it could."

The surgeons took their turns to be baffled but honoured the request. They believed they were stating the obvious outcome when they looked at the fresh x-rays. "The tumour is still there. We have to operate."

I felt like a failure: not even all the healers in North America could touch me. Later, my dad updated his understanding to reflect that what he had been shown must have been the amputated result: my body was cancer-free now.

"I don't know that I could grieve at the time," I said to my therapist. Even though I'd been seeing him for a few years, I still got uncomfortable admitting sorrow. I started to cry and was fighting it. "My dad was hell-bent on the power of ceremony, my mother was doing her best to be positive."

On the day of being admitted to the hospital, I woke and walked into our kitchen. A card waited for me on the counter. *To your new, healthy body.* From then on, the anniversary of my leg being amputated became "Peg Leg Day," a day of celebration. A day to honour that my life was saved.

"But I didn't hear anyone telling me that this was awful," I told the therapist. "That this was sad and terrifying. That I was losing something." I felt conflicted saying it even then, because I was lucky. I was so lucky that there was a cure. I was grateful and thought that gratitude should subsume all else. But recently I had been struggling with anger. I would lose my footing and feel anger. I tripped, and I felt anger. I got a sore on my stump, and I felt anger. I couldn't find a parking space close to my destination, and I felt anger. The grocery bags were too heavy to carry. The snow was too thick to walk through. Whenever I reached my limitations, I was overcome with frustration and bitterness.

"I don't want to hate part of myself," I said, struggling to find the clearer truth in that. My therapist did it for me. "It sounds like you already do hate it, though." And we waited while I cried.

"It may be if you could grieve the loss, you would feel less anger."

"And then what?" I asked. I couldn't imagine being on the other side.

"You would find out," he said. "But what I'm saying is you have a right to feel frustrated. You have a right to struggle with the complexity."

Ten days after my left leg was amputated above the knee, the staples were removed. What remained of my leg was swollen and tender. The doctor showed my mom and me how to wrap my stump in tensor bandages, overlapping and diagonal, to keep the swelling down. I wouldn't be able to be fitted for a prosthesis until the swelling subsided.

Learning to walk again was not instinctive. Three, four times a week I'd be at the rehab hospital getting fitted for a prosthesis. The process for the socket, at the time, was to make a plaster of Paris mould of the residual limb, which involved the prosthetist keeping their hands gripped in my groin while the plaster dried, to ensure the lip of the socket was shaped to later hold weight in the right places (under the ischial tuberosity, a.k.a sitting bone) and not in the wrong places (landing the body's weight in said groin with smarting results).

My first socket was a belt socket. I pulled on cotton or wool socks of varying ply over my stump (this allowed some flexibility for the post-surgery swelling and shrink) and slid the socket over my stump. Then I fastened the belt from one side of the socket around my waist to secure with Velcro to the front. The belt was lined with leather, which over the years would tan my waist brown where it rubbed. The skin that took my weight on the lip of the prosthesis would also be changed, rubbed to a tough leather, darker than any other part of my body.

First, trying to stand. Next, taking steps while holding on to bars. It wasn't at all like having two feet, learning to trust that something you couldn't feel would support your body. I felt my heel strike the ground not in my heel but in my hips and butt.

The day came when I was to try taking steps without the bars. My prosthetist held on to a strap tied around my torso;

she'd pull to keep me upright should I start to fall. Using my hands, I stood up from the stool that stayed in the middle of the barred walkway. My prosthetist wheeled the stool toward her and sat herself down.

"I promise I'll catch you!"

I didn't believe her.

I lifted my hands from the bars, though they stayed hovering and ready to grip. I lifted my right foot off the ground and took a small step forward. In the span of that small step, my prosthesis, my left side, that new floating feeling of weight-bearing, held me.

I shot a look up at my mom, beaming. For the second time in my life, I was learning to walk.

—◆—

My first junior high dance was only a year or so after I lost my leg. I purposefully didn't wear my prosthesis to school that day—it wasn't unusual for me to show up on crutches, as I didn't yet have the strength and endurance to wear my leg all day long. My lack of a left leg was impossible to miss without the prosthetic on. I was sure that if I didn't wear it, no one would ask me to dance. The prospect of being asked terrified me.

I sat giggling with my self-conscious preteen friends on a bench at the side of the gym while we watched the cool kids sway. Mr. D, the math teacher, kept our gang of wallflowers company. He was one of the youngest teachers at our school, a newlywed with a baby on the way, and managed often to balance authority with amity; he hadn't forgotten his own teen years.

Nathan, sweet, blond, chubby, warm, kind, funny, came toward us in a fit of youthful bravery. Each of the other girls on the bench sat upright, wondering who he was aiming for.

"Do you want to dance?"

I hadn't sat upright; I hadn't looked up. It took an elbow in the ribs to realize he was asking me. I balked.

"I don't have my leg on!"

He asked again. "Do you want to dance?" Hand outstretched.

I'd had a crush on him for so long. We'd briefly sat next to each other during Computers, and I'd studied how he brushed his long bangs from his face (with a move of both his hand and his head) more than anything on-screen. He got teased for his name, his size, his clothes, but his good-natured humour and quick comebacks kept him in the good graces of the jocks and extroverts. He was nicer than the lot of them.

I shook my head, *no*, as Mr. D chimed in, "Come ON! Dance with the boy!" Nathan shrugged it off and walked away. Mr. D widened his eyes at me, at my missed opportunity and Nathan's likely bruised ego. He liked Nathan and me—both misfits with aching hearts.

I've always regretted saying no. Saying yes could have changed everything in that horrible battlefield of adolescence.

I wore my leg to the next school dance and waited for Nathan to approach me. He never did. No one ever asked again, because that was the last time I went near a place anyone could.

In high school, I wore my prosthesis without any cosmetic cover, baring the black mechanics of the knee and shank for all to see. I felt defiant in it. I wanted people to know at a glance that I only had one leg. I got autographs on the socket. I painted the black surface and stuck stickers to it, including a blue and white accessibility symbol of a person in a wheelchair, a statement I found funny and ironic. When an innocent peer asked, "Are you required to wear that sticker?" I answered, dripping sarcasm and rolling eyes, "Yes, because it's not obvious otherwise that I'm disabled." The prosthesis was an extension of places like my bedroom and my locker, somewhere to assert and explore likes and personas.

But I was also poking a wound. I hated how the prosthesis looked and felt, awkward, cumbersome, at best uncomfortable but most often painful. I tripped and fell regularly, each time burning with embarrassment and frustration. I hated my difference and displayed it in part out of shame. *Look at me. I am grotesque.* I was trying to force acceptance.

In my early twenties, I wanted to pass for a two-legged person. I hid the mechanics under a carved foam cover to match the shape of my right leg and always wore pants. I was in disguise.

Though I kept it hidden, I remained conflicted: was my prosthesis part of my body or simply an accessory? I felt fiercely connected to it and protective—if I wasn't wearing my prosthesis and I saw someone else handle or move it, I was struck by a stab of discomfort. Wearing it often felt like a shoe that almost fit. With it off, I was unencumbered. Using crutches freed my lower limb but restricted my hands.

I could crawl, but that was impractical outside of my home. My prosthesis was both a part of my whole and external to it.

—◆—

Every time I said "Genium" out loud, I waved my hands and sang an "aaaah," the sound of angelic voices on rays of sunlight. The Genium was a famed prosthetic knee, one of the few on the market with a microprocessor. Salesmen flew from Salt Lake City to Vancouver to demonstrate the knee to me in person—and to install it without my clinic learning much about the top-secret software. Should I decide to purchase the awe-inspiring knee, my prosthetists would be educated, but until then, the technology remained gated. The group of sales reps stood around me, watching as my physiotherapist—the only other woman there—tried to keep my attention focused on what she was saying and away from the pitch of those interested in the sale.

The profile of the "calf" was larger than my own, designed to be "masculine" and appear muscular. There was no other benefit to its appearance. The thing that made my angel-hands sing: a person could ascend stairs step over step. In theory. It turned out, to walk step over step up stairs with the Genium required a constant commitment to obtaining and maintaining the strength it took to accomplish the feat—one that, even once I got to keep the knee for a trial two weeks and my physio and I met in my neighbourhood to experiment away from watching eyes, I could barely pull off.

I was courted by two other microprocessor knees: the Rheo 3 (with no angels singing or out-of-town salesmen) and the C-Leg, which was the most-installed microprocessor knee, my clinic told me, not without their own bias.

None of the microprocessor knees had been seriously on my radar months before. The C-Leg I had heard about for years, but each time I researched possible funding, I discovered there was none, other than private investment, for the cost of forty thousand dollars. I pushed considering a microprocessor knee from my mind, knowing I could never afford one.

Then, in a waiting room, a congenital leg amputee told me she'd had a trial with the C-Leg. "It's what I imagine having two legs feels like," she said. The statement piqued my interest in a new way. I could remember what two legs felt like, and I wondered if I'd agree with her. I decided to try the knee, simply for the experience. The trial began that December, and because of Christmas, I got to extend my time with the knee from the usually granted two weeks to a full month.

For the third time in my life, I learned to walk. To use the microprocessor knee, I had to put aside what I had practised for over twenty years with my previous prosthetic knees: I had to let it bend and hold my weight. Every knee before it had to be in a locked position before bearing weight; otherwise, it would collapse and I would fall. I fell at least once a week, never subtly, and never without bruising my "good" knee. The microprocessor, I learned, senses when it's bearing weight and provides resistance in response. Not falling was glorious.

I spent a lot of time during the trial learning and unlearning with the microprocessor knee. I stood at the top of a five-step staircase in the rehab hospital, my physiotherapist at the bottom. I understood how the technology worked—we had already tested it standing.

"Just walk down the stairs. Step over step. Do it," she said. Counter to instincts yelling, "YOU WILL FALL, DON'T DO IT," I lifted my right leg, shifted my weight to my left and felt the knee bend slowly, bearing my weight, lowering me onto the next step. I repeated the motion, astonished, for the remaining four steps and launched myself into my physio's arms. I had to hug her; the experience was a revelation. My body remembered the sensation of descending stairs. One foot over the other was like looking at long-lost photographs, an ecstatic recollection.

Returning the C-Leg after a month, I felt like I was turning into a pumpkin. I posted a photograph to Facebook saying so, and for a lot of folks in my community, it was the first time they'd realized I didn't have a leg. It was also, for many, the first time they'd considered walking down stairs as extraordinary. I didn't expect the response, but as the comments started rolling in, a proposal: Let's crowdfund a knee!

Five years had passed since Ford died, and I believe the helplessness people felt in supporting me for that loss and the loss of Emmett was given an antidote by this action they could take. We called it the Kneeraiser, and when it launched, we raised fifteen thousand dollars in less than two days. Another ten thousand dollars came in over the coming weeks. The campaign was managed by Susan, my lifelong friend, who had danced with me just days before my leg was amputated. Coordination became her near full-time job.

The large sums were meaningful, but more affecting were the donations of ten or twenty dollars from musicians and artists I knew could barely afford it. With the money waiting to be spent, I did a one-month trial with the Rheo 3 knee, preferred it to the C-Leg and wrote the biggest cheque of my life. I would say later, "It's the knee that folk music bought," because it was through the Kneeraiser I discovered my place in the music community—that I truly felt their love and support. Above all, I felt the love of Susan and the strength of our friendship, which by now spanned decades.

I didn't know how to say thank you. I wanted to celebrate. I decided to no longer be in disguise.

"How do we make an affordable version of this?" I said, holding up my cellphone to my prosthetists, showing them photos of a hand-painted prosthesis adorned with winding flowers from toe to hip. I'd never seen anything like it—beautiful. The answer was simple: lamination. I found an upholstery fabric that conjured the petals and leaves I loved on the painted leg, and the prosthetists wrapped it around the socket. They made a hard shell for the lower half of my prosthesis and wrapped it in the fabric, too.

The result was striking. From far away it appeared to be a full-leg tattoo and has been mistaken for one. Up close, the mechanics, the hinge, are clear. The great Vancouver drag queen Joan-E once said at a drag bingo night, "If you can't hide it, decorate it." Her words came thundering back when I saw my flower leg for the first time. I wondered if I'd over-estimated my confidence. The first public place I walked in, flowers bared, was a Shoppers Drug Mart. I sensed people looking at me in the aisles, at the checkout, and I felt rejection and missed dances and assumptions of injury bubbling up. I reminded myself of how beautiful I thought the painted inspiration was. I assured myself I could feel that beautiful, too.

Over the following weeks, my comfort level grew; confidence burgeoned. "Petal to the mettle," a friend coined, and the flower leg became an avenue to re-examine my disability. Joan-E was right: there's plenty we can't hide or change. In getting the flower leg, I was not just making my disability visible, I was putting up a neon sign pointing to it. That boldness began to make me feel like I had a superpower. The old, embarrassed "oh, sorry!" reply when I told someone I only had one leg was replaced with excitement and interest—people saying they thought the flower leg was gorgeous or asking how it was made or how it worked. No longer questions about how I lost my leg; almost exclusively appreciation for the artfulness of it.

That has continued, though occasionally people still get it wrong.

Waiting in line for a bus, I had headphones in; I was wearing a skirt, so my prosthetic leg was visible. A man approached and motioned for me to take off my headphones. I complied and waited for him to speak.

"I just want to say, I think you're an inspiration."

"Sorry?" I said.

He pointed to my leg. "It's incredible, what you're doing."

Waiting for the bus? I thought. "Um, thanks," I said. I imagined that he thought it was a feat for me to leave the house, to be seen in public. Hot tip: before you tell a person with a disability they're an inspiration, make sure they're doing something actually inspirational.

Once, at the airport, I parked in the accessible spot in front of arrivals, my parking permit clearly hanging off the rear-view mirror. The parking attendant on duty, who shoos idling cars out of the accessible spot and the rest of the lane intended only for pick-ups, shouted at me from a few cars back, "You can't park there!"

"I have the permit!" I said, pointing to my car.

"But you're not disabled!" he said.

By then, he'd caught up to me and we were face to face.

"I am disabled," I said, not wanting to say anything else.

"You don't look it," he said.

"I only have one leg," I conceded. He looked me up and down before he gave his own "harrumph" of concession and walked away.

"Well, you don't look ignorant, but you are," I said, wishing I'd thought of it while he was still in earshot. I wanted to follow him and ask if the risk of my using the permit illegally was greater than the risk of him making such an uneducated statement. I wanted him to understand that I have the permit so I don't have to explain things, so I don't have to ask for access and help.

In the parking lot of a grocery store, Susan and I were loading bags into the back of her car for a weekend getaway. A man approached. "Can I ask you about your leg?"

"Sure!" I replied, by now used to questions about how the floral cover got made, is it painted, can they take a picture for their cousin who's also an amputee, and so on. I glanced at Susan to acknowledge we might be slightly delayed due to my rock star–amputee status. She smiled.

"Were you born this way, or did you lose your leg?" he said. I don't mind the question, though it wasn't what I expected.

"It was amputated when I was a kid. I was lucky, though, it was the cure for my cancer," I said, giving my usual spiel. "It's a good thing."

He nodded. "So you were born whole. The Lord intended you to be whole," he said. Stunned, I didn't interrupt him straightaway. He continued to tell me the story of a local preacher. "He was a preacher in the 1800s who lost his leg. And he prayed so hard and long that the Lord would return his leg to him, that one night in prayer circle, the Lord grew him a leg right there in front of his parishioners. They witnessed his leg shoot right out of his pant leg in front of them!"

"Ummm." I was searching for words and looked at Susan, whose widened eyes darted between the man and me.

"Are you a Christian?" he said.

"No," I said with please-stop-talking clarity.

"Well, if you prayed to the Lord—"

"Sir, I am whole. I have no problem with how my body is," I began.

He put up his hands and started to walk away, calling back, "Miracles do happen." Susan and I got in the car, and as she drove, I said everything else I wanted him to know: how dare he presume I want to be changed.

———

It was a first date. Tea. "I'm a swing dancer," he said. He joked that I'm part robot, the flashing green light on my microprocessor knee blinking in agreement. "I bet you could dance."

I delighted in this stranger's confidence. The flower leg and the new knee it encased were only a few months old.

The city I was in was the newest of all—just a couple weeks had passed since I arrived in Toronto from Vancouver. My plan: Step away from the years of heartache by stepping into a different environment, take a break from reminders everywhere, try not to burn everything to the ground. Better yet, try something new.

Going on dates seemed in line with the plan. After tea, we had manhattans on his city-view balcony. He suggested we start with blues dancing, and I told myself, "You never have to see him again" as a reason to try it. Why else had I moved to a big city but to say yes?

We stood and began. My spine straightened to the feel of his hand on my back, a quick breath in. I tried not to reveal how I could stand there just for that. Touch.

"It's basically like high school slow dancing," he said.

"I never high school slow danced," I said, keeping to myself the failed junior high dance experience and my staunch avoidance of all dance opportunities since. At nightclubs with friends, I'd drink and chat by the bar, the one to watch coats and bags while the others took to the dance floor. At weddings, I'd engage deeply in conversation with the great-aunts and uncles on the sidelines.

As he tried to teach me, I couldn't stop laughing, I couldn't not look up at his face, attempting to follow his verbal direction, untrained and unconfident about following his physical cues. I couldn't help saying again, "I've never done anything like this." It seemed simple enough, the dancing with another person business. What had taken me so long?

He told me I was funny (I imagined he meant foolish), while suggesting I rest my head on his chest, close my eyes and follow by feel.

"I might ask if I can kiss you if we keep dancing," he said. We stopped.

"Saturday, dancing?" he texted days later. I replied with how much I wanted to, how much it scared me and "If you can laugh with me, not at, I'd like that."

"I can do that."

Saturday arrived, and with Susan on speaker phone, I deliberated between the only two dresses I'd brought on the move. "You can leave if it's awful," she said in pep talk mode. "And if anyone judges you, fuck them."

At Dovercourt House, the dancing date destination, I felt anxious and out of place. "I'm paying your cover in case you hate this," he said. I said he had to hold my hand. I took one of his in my two and pressed it to my belly, where nervousness kicked back. We got a bravery drink and sat on the sidelines. He knew every other person there. "Hiiiii!" they all squealed. He described to me who he liked dancing with most, who was awkward, who got too grindy. He taught me some etiquette: "People are going to ask you to dance. If you want to say no, you can either say, 'I'm only dancing with this person'—but then you really have to dance with just me—or you can say, 'I'm sitting this song out,' but then make sure you actually do. Or maybe you're never going to come back, in which case who cares what they think, say whatever you want."

It felt like a dream sequence—part high school gym, part *Dirty Dancing*. Once our drink was done, he asked, "You ready?" and we were up, stepping off that cliff, a first dance after all those years of purposeful wallflowering. I laughed through most of it. I felt like a sore thumb, awkward and different from the rest. And it felt great. We sat down.

He danced with someone else. I watched the room, sure I was still dreaming.

We went upstairs to the swing floor where a live band was playing, and it was once more out of a movie to me, hazy, lights low. We got another round of drinks, and he introduced me to a few friends; he danced with a couple of them. It was so fun to watch, legs kicking all over the place, spinning, swirling, some of it was so fast. His friends told me what they liked about him and asked, "How do you know him?"

I didn't, really.

We headed back to the blues floor, and while he danced with someone, a gentlemen of over sixty years (mostly the crowd was under forty), German (I learned) and straddling the fine line between charming and smarmy, asked to me dance. Or, more accurately, finagled the conversation so it seemed like I asked him. It turned out he hadn't noticed my leg. While dancing I said, "I'm new at this," to which he replied, "I can tell."

"I only have one leg, so ..."

"Wait, what?" The familiar surprise that by now only made me smile. My superpower.

He was a more forceful lead than my date, and in some ways easier to follow because of it, his hands pushing harder to guide our dance. "Can I ask you an intimate question?" He leaned in and continued, "Do you water-ski?"

"No," I replied tentatively, wondering if the "intimate" part was yet to come.

"Good, because blues dancing is not like water-skiing. You need to be up on your toes."

"I don't have toes."

The song ended. I thanked him and reached for my date, who was nearby. "I was worried about you," he laughed. We danced again, and I danced with others. I lost count of the times. I felt electric in my limbs, hands, legs, listening. I thought of Huz.

"I'm not going to call it your stump. It's your little leg." Huz was the first person I let love my little leg, let know every scar, the indent in the femur, the calluses, the roughness, the softness most of all. What would he say if he had seen me that night? He knew my old limits best. He would have been as amazed as I was at the changes the new microprocessor knee made, at the change being alone in a new city had made to me. I imagined him proud of me, happy for me. I pictured him at the side of the room, his silhouette that I could draw in the dark, and saw him feeling left out of some part of my life again.

In the haze of sweat and blues music, what I loved most (almost) was having my fingers intertwined in someone else's while they led me to the dance floor, into a sea of swaying people. Anticipation. Suggestion. Every hint from the lead's fingers, *this way, here*, sank in, and my body replied, *yes*. Each time I was surprised I knew the word in that context. How long I'd been heavy, how long I'd waited on the sidelines, hoping to be asked for this dance. That night, I loved my shape and how unique it was among the others. That night, I didn't resent the physical pain that came with the exertion, I simply took it in stride.

Stepping into the night air, we walked to find a cab. I was giddy and spent, and, as of that moment, I was a dancer: a shapeshifter still.

CHAPTER 9 SANIBE

At the base of my neck, a scar. A thin crescent moon shape twice made. First by a thyroidectomy and second, hours later, by an emergency procedure to address an arterial bleed—also referred to by Susan as "that time you were partially decapitated." Susan, always with a flair for humour and drama, was again by my side.

The thyroidectomy had been postponed several times, by me. Because the surgery came with a risk of injuring my voice, I first wanted to record another album, my fourth, with the voice I knew well. Then I wanted to tour the album once with that voice. So I kept asking for more time. My surgeon didn't understand. He was considered the top surgeon in his field, but like many doctors and specialists before him, he lacked warmth or even much interest in what I wanted. He was most often indifferent, and occasionally acted as if I were imposing on him with my questions and concerns. Surgeons are usually the most egregious at displaying indifference. I get it: their job is to cut things out and remaining emotionless helps them do that effectively. But it can make interacting with them exhausting.

"So we'll do it once you get back from your little trip," Dr. Top Surgeon said.

"It's not a trip, it's a tour," I said. "It's my work."

Friends and family expressed concern that I was delaying too long. The trouble with moving forward was the diagnosis: the multiple large and very slowly growing lumps on my thyroid could not be confirmed as cancerous. There was a fifty-fifty chance they were, and even then, "We're not talking capital-C cancer, here," Dr. Top Surgeon had stated a couple of years before. "Not like lung or breast cancer, where every day is of the essence." Depending on how you looked at it, I had already been unlucky with cancer— getting bone cancer and losing my leg to it. As the lumps at the base of my neck grew larger, I wore more and more scarves, covering myself against the double take some folks would make at the large bulge. Being self-conscious about how they looked was one thing. But as my tour approached, I started to notice them when I swallowed; it felt as if a hard bead were going down with every bite or gulp. The concern the lumps might be cancerous became moot with this impact: they, and my thyroid with them, needed to be removed as soon as I returned.

On the day, it was not Dr. Top Surgeon, with whom I'd had all previous appointments, but his Fellow who would perform the procedure. I briefly worried that I wasn't getting The Best, despite not liking The Best, but this doctor had a kindness to him, the exact thing Dr. Top Surgeon lacked. The surgery went off without a hitch, and Susan came to the hospital to greet me as I recovered, echoing the days in our childhood she'd visit me in my hospital room. She knows me well in physical recovery. I was ready to try to eat something after a day without food. It's not uncommon to vomit after having anaesthetic, and with my surgeries in the past, I'd learned it can take a few tries to determine if the food will stay down or not. Susan helped me sit up in bed and start simply, by taking a few spoonfuls of yogurt and applesauce. It wasn't long before I discovered my body wasn't ready for it.

Susan held the bowl under my mouth as I puked. When it was over, I felt a sudden, rising pain in my neck. "It hurts," I said.

"I know," she said, soothingly. When I placed my hand on my neck, I could feel it swelling under my fingers. I breathed in, and to my surprise, made an audible rasping gasp; it was increasingly difficult to breathe. Susan immediately thought I was having an allergic reaction, so quick was the swelling of my neck.

We scrambled for the call bell, only to discover it wasn't working. Susan ran into the hallway yelling for help. When a nurse arrived, she determined instantly it was "a bleed." She yanked the call bell cord out of the wall—a move I had not learned before, despite my long hospital career, that triggers an emergency alarm. More nurses arrived. One slammed ice packs on my neck, and a ripped bag soaked my hospital gown with a gush of icy water. The kind surgeon was paged.

The room was frenzied until he arrived. Susan observing closely from the foot of my bed. Nurses running in and out. Two student nurses standing idly, awkward and, to Susan's horror, giggling. But when the surgeon entered, everyone stopped, at the ready. "You have a bleed," he confirmed as he went methodically through the motions of opening the sterile materials brought to my bedside.

"It's an artery, from the looks of it," he said, referring to the rate of the swelling. "I'm going to have to open your neck to alleviate the pressure." With the force of vomiting, an artery, cut and then soldered during the surgery, had burst open. It's not common for that to happen, and arterial bleeds are less likely than venous ones.

As the surgeon and nurses worked around me, I listened without speaking. The pain was sharp in my neck, and I was dizzy with the intensity of it, like I was being drained from head to toe. It felt as if a hundred fingers were prodding my neck. They had given me oxygen to assist my breathing—that difficulty had frightened me—and were discussing what kind of pain management they could administer. Many drugs weren't possible as, once the immediate threat was eliminated, I would have to be taken back to the operating room, and medications could interfere with anaesthetic I'd receive there.

The surgeon undid the stitches he'd put in my neck to pull open my skin and muscle. With every gasp of pain I made, he looked me in the eye, making his moves in tandem with my experience. I clocked his steadiness and felt reassured. I looked at Susan as she stood watching the scene unfold. For a moment, all the times I had watched my son Ford be cared for through medical emergencies came back to me. That is what I'd looked like, I realized, seeing her scared and feeling her love for me. *I probably won't die because there are all these people here to fix this*, I thought, *but I do need to get through the pain.* Another tug at the flesh of my neck slammed my awareness back into my body. Fuck, it really hurt. *Maybe I am dying.*

With my neck re-opened, the surgeon's fingers pulled clots out of the cavity, and blood poured down my chest. There was release, the pressure in my neck instantly subsiding. With it went some of the immediate fear, though I remained in shock. I was propped up in the bed, and an operating room was prepared. Soon, I was wheeled back into surgery. The surgeon helped me lie back on the operating table. It hurt so much to move. My bloodied hospital gown fell off my shoulders, baring my chest, but I didn't care. They placed the black rubber mask over my face to administer the anaesthetic, and I was out. They repeated the work of sealing the cut artery shut.

Two weeks after the ordeal, I met with the Fellow who had performed both surgeries and Dr. Top Surgeon. The pathology confirmed the lumps on my neck had been cancerous. I wasn't surprised and felt almost numb to the news, too affected by the recent surgery.

"I thought I might die," I said to them.

"You definitely weren't going to die. We might have had to trach you if things got worse," the Fellow said, then paused when he saw how shaken I still was. He changed course, and his kindness came to the fore. "I was scared, too. This happens maybe once every three hundred times, and when I got the page, I was so sorry to hear it was you."

He remembered my medical history. My kids. I smiled at him with gratitude. His senior didn't respond as warmly. "Well, don't complain, because we cured you of cancer," he said.

"That's not the point," I protested, but Dr. Top Surgeon didn't hear. He had left the room.

"I know," said the Fellow. I smiled to thank him again.

—•—

Christa is the name I use most often, but I have another: my traditional name, Sanibe. SAY-nee-bay. Sanibe means Singing Woman.

In my Cree culture—in many Indigenous cultures—traditional names or spirit names are given in ceremony, and they relate to a person's role in the community. The names speak to our gifts, and they speak to our duty to use those gifts. I was given mine when I was two, though Sanibe is not actually a Cree word, because the Elder who gave me my name was Arapaho. We were on his territory, and you work with what you've got.

At my naming ceremony the Elder, Raymond, told my family, "She's going to sing a lot, and she's going to talk a lot." And that is a story I heard over and over when I was growing up. "Oh, Raymond told us, she's going to sing a lot, and she's going to talk a lot." I loved that story, and when that story was told, I felt loved.

I don't know if I grew into the name or if the name just happened to fit, but I have written songs for as long as I can remember. The first that exists in memory, I wrote when I was seven or eight:

She's a mermaid swimming through the sea
Flipping her tail here and there and singing beautifully

Oh I wish I could be a mermaid
I wish I could swim like one too
But I know no matter how hard I wish
I could never be a kind of fish

I shared that first song with no one. My writing improved over the years, but my reluctance to make any of it public was steadfast. Despite being in choir and high school musicals, I was shy—terrified, really—of performing solo. At a karaoke night with colleagues from my first teenaged coffee shop job, I started to shake when I took my turn and sang "True Colours." The thought of performing something I had written was even scarier. At the same time, I had a deep desire to do it; I dreamed of standing on a stage and singing my own songs to an audience. In the daydream, I shone. In reality, I retreated. After high school, when I began working in the film industry, I kept that dream, as well as my being Sanibe, to myself.

———◆———

There used to be a hostel in Amsterdam called The Last Waterhole. Above the entrance hung their sign with the problematic and inexplicable image of a Plains Indian man in a war bonnet. Inside, the main floor housed a dark and bustling bar, pool tables and a stage graced nightly by live rock music. Upstairs, rooms of bunk beds and shared bathrooms with no gender divide. It was dirty and cheap and, on my first trip to Europe, the only place available thanks to my arrival dates coinciding with a long weekend in the UK. Thus, when I stepped into the bar alone and looking to strike up conversation, The Last Waterhole was also filled with Brits and Scots.

I attached myself to a few who were partying in Amsterdam for the weekend. I was in the first days of what would be six weeks of travelling solo. I'd arrived starry-eyed and ill-prepared for the realities of backpacking through Europe alone and with a disability, but the group who invited me to join them had all travelled enough to give me much-needed encouragement and tips, like taking night trains to avoid paying for accommodation.

On the second night, I sat in a back room at The Last Waterhole among some other travellers with Darryl, my favourite Scot of the bunch. It was late, after last call, and the final song rocked the stage. Most of us had returned to the hostel after numerous other stops in our Amsterdam adventures. An acoustic guitar was passed around the circle, and folks took turns singing cover songs. Darryl sang a David Gray song, "This Year's Love," and I delighted in singing harmonies.

"Do you play?" he asked when the guitar reached me.

"A little," I said, though it had only been a few months since I started lessons, and I'd never played or sung in front of anyone by myself. But the late hour, the anonymity and the haze of the evening gave me enough courage to play one of the small songs I had composed, a love song for my recent ex and first love, Kathy. Shaking a little at first, by the time the song was done, I felt calm. A moment of stillness hung in the air with my last notes; people had been listening in silence. Darryl broke the suspense. "Aye," he said with a long sigh, and everyone followed with applause. I had always

known I was Singing Woman, but it was in the moment
between me stopping and Darryl speaking that I embod-
ied it. I became a singer. In those few enchanted seconds, I
knew I wanted to make music more than a secret hobby, to
have many more seconds just like that. After I said goodbye
to Darryl and his friends, I missed my train to Munich, sitting on the platform to write:

> *He tells me that I'm solid, says, "Will you come my way?"*
> *I wonder if he knew me better what else he'd have to say*
> *It's a kiss to wake me up and a hand to help me down*
> *I am giddy with my freedom, I am warming to my sound*
>
> *And I sound like "go," so here I go*

When I got home, I was overflowing with new songs and
nurturing a budding confidence to share them. It took my
year-long move to England to be able to, but that night in
Amsterdam had changed my course. Over time, singing
songs became my work and source of income, though in
the fits and starts set by the lives and deaths of my children.
Music was also my survival through those losses.

Pounding a piano was especially cathartic. I stopped
caring if the neighbours could hear: I would bang the keys,
expelling anguish through my fingers, singing until I cried
and then crying until I collapsed, spent. Songs are my teachers. They move through me like dreams: veiled retellings
of my waking experiences. I see details revealed in songs
I could not have found through any other means, and I
have learned a lot about myself through them. Sometimes
immediately, sometimes years later when it dawns on

me: Oh, *that's* what that was about. For this reason, there are songs I've written that no one has ever heard; no one needs to.

The songs I did record and perform were the ones that transcended my most private moments, the ones I could invite people to see themselves in. Through telling my stories to a new audience every night, I felt seen and heard in turn. With grief in particular, those moments with audiences made me feel less alone.

"I lost a son," a woman told me after a show in Winnipeg. "Matthew." We hugged, and I promised to remember him. "My husband died last year," another woman told me through tears during the break at a show in Saint John, New Brunswick. "Walter, he was called." I promised to remember him too. I learned to focus on one person at a time when others were waiting to buy CDs or say hello, to be ready for those moments of mutual visibility.

After a while, I began to dedicate one song a night onstage to the most recent person I'd been told about. Most often they were children who'd died. Bereaved parents found me as though they could see me in the dark. (I could see them too.)

Sometimes connection occurred simply through the wordless magic of music. Onstage, there was always an instant when I knew I had the audience—and they had me. I could never predict when that would happen. Sometimes, it was in the first notes sung; often it wasn't until the third or fourth song, and occasionally it took longer. But each time, it was like finding a groove, like walking in step, like turning a key, even like falling in love. Performing music, to me, was like asking, "Know what I mean?" and feeling the reply: "Yes."

Hearts on both sides opened; there's no less cheesy way to describe it. On my side of the microphone, I felt it in the silences, in the applause, in an audible gasp from someone listening intently. If I could see the audience, I knew it from their faces.

For a long time, until I had new things to hold on to, those moments of connection with an audience kept me alive. As I sang about my experiences, I would feel people stitching their own lives into the fabric, seeing themselves in me. Of that exchange, I wrote:

> *I don't need an answer, I just need to talk*
> *But my mouth is a cocktail of lemon and chalk*
> *And it burns*
> *I don't need a destination, I just need to walk*
> *I need to gather my thoughts and take stock of my words*
>
> *Give me music—I could use it*
>
> *Sing for me—like all you speak is poetry*
> *Like nobody here knows us*
> *Sing for me—like your life depends on melody*
> *And I'll join in on the chorus*

Someone asked me recently about the loss of my children: "How are you okay?" It was hard to answer. Sometimes I'm okay, and sometimes I'm not. But I replied, "Time passing helps, and singing and writing helps, too." This is the reciprocal part of being Sanibe—the name speaks to what I can give, but it has also been a huge part of what I've received.

The keyboard in my home was under a south-facing window. The first time I sat in the sunlit spot after the thyroidectomy, I let my fingers start. They sank into the keys, playing slow, solid chords. I was nervous to try singing; my vocal cords had not been damaged in the surgery, thankfully, but the impact of the bleed and successive surgery still reverberated in my body and voice. Breathing in, I launched into a simple scale and heard an unfamiliar voice, a weakened voice, airy, pitchy and delivering truncated notes when it could hold long notes before.

I still sounded like me, but so very different. My fingers instinctively lifted from the keys. Fear that my voice had been irreparably changed flooded my quiet house. I knew intellectually it was early days and my voice would recover, but the stark change rattled my body and spirit. I stepped away from the keyboard.

As weeks passed, my range and capacity improved but remained decreased from my pre-surgery voice. The hardest part was that I would unpredictably hit off-key notes. My near-perfect pitch had always been a point of pride, and now my voice, which I had known so intimately, felt like an untamed creature. This thing that had been truly inherent, easy and pleasurable was gone.

My heart ached. I had lost part of who I was—again. This new sound, this difference, was the absence of what I had known before. I had one small gig to get through shortly after the surgery, which I managed, and then I stopped performing. I didn't know what to do with my voice; I resented its limitations. How could I be Singing Woman if I wasn't singing songs?

Eight months after the surgery, I was invited to perform at an event in Port Hope, Ontario. I knew I'd been invited to present my music, but I wasn't ready to sing in front of people with this new, broken voice. I scheduled a breakfast meeting with the event organizers to talk about options, and as I looked in the mirror before the meeting, the words I'd heard all those times came to mind: "She's going to sing a lot, and she's going to talk a lot." And I remembered: I loved that story, and when that story was told, I felt loved.

For the first time ever, I granted the second half of that teaching its own significance. I'd always understood "she's going to sing a lot"; that part was obvious. I'd thought "she's going to talk a lot" just meant I was chatty. But now it occurred to me it could also relate to what my role is in this world and how I can serve my community. It could be part of everything my traditional name asked and gave me to do. I could talk. As I considered this for the first time, I felt a wave of relief.

On the night of the event, I walked out from the wings with neither guitar in hand nor piano to turn to. This was a first for me.

I approached the mic and blinked at the spotlights. I imagined kindness waiting in the silent auditorium that greeted me. And I spoke. My voice hung in the room. I was nervous without the company of an instrument, but I pressed my feet onto the floor and took the same deep breath I've always taken. I told the ears and hearts there what I'd been trying to come to terms with: after my voice was injured, I hadn't known who Sanibe could be anymore, and I'd been grappling with my identity. I told them I'd never just spoken on a stage before. I told them about loss, resilience and hope. I read some very early pages from this book, part of Emmett's birth story. I moved my arms through the air as I spoke, expressing the rhythm and cadence of my words instead of moving my hands across a piano. My nervousness subsided, and before my talk was done, I found the bits of silence once filled by instruments to be a beautiful sound.

Speaking to an audience felt raw and new. But it was also familiar. It turns out talking conveys the same invitation to listeners that singing always did: the invitation to be less alone.

I am Singing Woman, with or without a song.

CHAPTER 10 WHICH GHOSTS ARE YOURS

In the first few months after Huz left, I'd begun to long for an escape. The apartment walls had witnessed too much. Even painted white, I could see our years of suffering captured in them. I rearranged furniture, slept in different corners, tried to make something new of the old place but couldn't. Each neighbour who said hello to me by the mailboxes seemed to pity me, and I wanted to be free of their memories too.

Toronto wasn't without ghosts. It was the city where Ford had lived half of his life. Toronto was the city where he'd died. In the years before that, it was a city I'd known through visiting family and friends, a city full of bustle and things to do. After his death, it was a city I was afraid of, since around every corner was a reminder.

From Vancouver, I could believe that Ford was still in Toronto. It was magical thinking: *He is just at the hospital, the nurses who love him are with him. He is okay.* Whenever I visited Toronto, I would feel a pull to the hospital: *I should be there.* And then the reality: *But he is not.* Moving to the city meant facing that pull and challenging that belief—a painful exercise, but I needed it. I needed to know, really know, that he was gone. The suspension hurt too much.

Toronto was also home to a few of my dearest friends; I would not stray too far from myself with them in reach. I decided to give myself a year—one year of trying new things, one year of saying yes to new opportunities, one year of indulging in invention, one year away from Vancouver with the hope I'd determine if I was just running away or was truly ready to leave.

Public transit alone proved to be exposure therapy. Each subway stop had a story tied to Ford's life, and every time I stepped onto a platform I relived it. I tried to create small, new stories—I'd look at the tile, the advertising, and think about the date, the year, where I'd been that day so far and where I was going. There were places I didn't attempt to augment; I avoided the street the hospital was on at all costs. If I failed to redirect a cab and it turned up the street, I'd look away or close my eyes and, as in the childhood game of passing a graveyard, lift my feet and hold my breath. As when Ford was alive there, I could and still can sense the nearness of that place, even with my eyes shut, and I cry when I'm near it. Sometimes those tears carry little emotion, but my body simply can't forget, and I can't stop it from remembering.

—•—

I arrived in Toronto in May with two suitcases, my guitar and my keyboard. Everything else stayed in Vancouver in my old apartment, sublet for a year to buy time without losing the place I'd loved for so long, that I wondered if I could love again. Without seeing it in person, I took a room in a house in Toronto with five others. I thought a house full of people would buffer me against loneliness in a new city and promote The Exploration of Something New. That succeeded only slightly. It turned out avoiding telling five people that I was recently separated and almost as recently bereaved of two children was a challenge. I didn't plan to lie about these things, but I had hoped to take a break from talking about them. Also, the other five housemates were young, much younger than I was, some living away from their parents for the first time, and there was too much distance between our experiences. They were kind, smart, interesting people in a drastically different stage of life. I felt out of place—not what I was looking for in a new hometown, or even in a one-year adventure.

After six weeks, I decided to sublet a friend's room for the summer. From there, another sublet, this time an apartment on my own. The solo space wasn't lonely but a welcome exhale into every corner. I relished taking up all the space. I sang loudly, I left the dishes, I walked around naked, I ate chips sitting on the floor. The apartment was on a busy street in a lively neighbourhood, and just waiting for the streetcar gave me the comfort of proximity to people. I explored Toronto as fully as possible—places, neighbourhoods, venues and people.

Dating with the flower leg was a new landscape. Online, I experimented with including photos of my leg or mentioning it beforehand, with mixed results.

"I'm the one with the floral prosthetic leg," I messaged to one first date when plans to meet were being finalized.

"Oh!" she replied, admitting later she'd considered cancelling.

"Oh, wow, your leg!" another first date said after our initial hellos. With this potential paramour, I had not drawn attention to my leg in advance, though the photos in my profile displayed it. I could tell he was caught off guard.

"It's in my pictures," I explained, regretting that I felt apologetic.

"I didn't notice," he said, visibly uncomfortable. We finished our drinks, and later I wished I had been brave enough to call it a night sooner. Instead, I indulged his polite conversation until it was reasonable for us to say goodbye.

Of course, there was the opposite effect: the leg, and my disability, got fetishized and objectified, which I was also not looking for. I was searching, not for someone who was fluent with disability, necessarily, but one who could be curious with kindness.

Dating in my mid-thirties meant I wasn't the only one who was divorced, or at least on the other side of a long-term relationship. As with my disability, I experimented with whether and when to share that I had two children. Here, too, I searched for kindness.

—◆—

Since I talk with my hands, you'll eventually see a tattoo of a skeleton key on my right wrist. As a young teen, in a spate of boredom during one of my stays with my dad, I went into his garage (he always had one, no matter where he moved: a shed, a garage, a place for his tools) and opened every Folgers coffee can that lined the shelves. These cans, red and green with white and gold letters, stored nails, screws, bolts, wire, batteries and, as I discovered in one, keys. In that can was a silver skeleton key. I liked how it looked and tucked it into my pocket. On the same visit, I took several red plaid flannel shirts from my dad's closet, all perfectly enormous over my early-nineties-grunge-hopeful loose jeans and each a perfect backdrop for the skeleton key, which I wore on a ribbon around my neck. When it no longer suited my style to wear it as an accessory, I moved the key to my key chain.

The first house I lived in after I left my mother's had old glass doors between each room with brass doorknobs and keyholes. On a whim, I slid the skeleton key into one keyhole after another and turned it with a click. That it fit seemed magical. Any friend who came by had to witness the lucky key locking and unlocking doors. From that first home, I would move on to many others, shared and alone. The magical skeleton key lived on my keychain next to whatever else unlocked the doors of my life at the time.

After ten months in Toronto, I needed to move out of the lovely solo sublet. My few belongings would go into storage while I went down to Nashville to record my fourth album. I still didn't know if I planned to make Toronto my home. If I was going to stay there, I'd find a new place to live when I returned. Not a sublet, but ideally something more permanent.

With only a few days left in the city, I went out to an appointment on a windy, cold day. Upon my return, I stepped into the building's lobby and reached for my keys—they weren't in my pocket. I searched the ground. I retraced my steps in a swelling snowstorm. I phoned each place I'd been and the businesses near each bus stop where I'd waited. For days after, I'd check the transit lost and found. Gone.

My first thought was not of being locked out but of my skeleton key. A picture of it flashed in my mind, causing a greater ache than I could have anticipated. As the hours passed, I ached for it still. The souvenir of my father, the memory of my first home, the constant it had been through every place I'd called home for twenty years.

But at the same time, the loss seemed fitting. At that point in my life, without even a city to belong to, in the wake of every other loss, of course the symbol of home I'd carried through it all would go. It was just a key, but I had cherished it. When it disappeared into Toronto's tumult, I surrendered to feeling ungrounded.

A month later, I got the tattoo: a reminder that home will only ever be, truly, in my skin. It's inked on the inside of my wrist, and I imagine that with a shake of my hand, the key could slide into my fingers, ready to unlock any door.

—◆—

My fourth album was the first not tied to a pregnancy or a birth. Instead, it was filled with divorce and change. The working title shifted from things like *Everyday Heartache* to *Ordinary Crisis*. Writing a break-up album seemed a songwriter cliché, easy territory considering the losses I'd mined on previous albums. Everyone knows the woe of a relationship ending.

During the week the album was recorded in Nashville, I decided not to move back to Vancouver. Time was up—one year had passed, and the terms of subletting my old apartment stated I must move out or move back. Notice had to be given. I was neither ready to return to Vancouver nor ready to leave Toronto. I wanted more time to make up my mind, and that desire defaulted to picking Toronto for the next little while. Of my slow decision, I said to someone in Nashville, "I've been such a long time leaving," and the album got its name.

In my "deciding" year away, I'd spent Emmett and Ford's birthdays and death anniversaries knitting or sewing small gifts that I then mailed to friends to take to my sons' shared grave. One friend called me from the cemetery and described everything he could see, feel, hear—the blue skies, the warm air, the nearby traffic—and then set up a FaceTime call in front of their columbarium marker, stepped out of earshot and left me to talk to the site. Visiting their grave was one of the things I missed most about Vancouver, and one of the things that pulled against me leaving there for good.

On the day I arrived in Vancouver to start the Great Purge and Move, I went to their grave in person. As I approached, I saw a collection of new items since the last photos anyone had sent me—toy cars, chestnuts, a piece of driftwood with Ford's name burned in. These offerings always move me. I fear sometimes that I will be the only one who remembers them. But their father, aunts, grandparents remember, of course; the evidence is a welcome reminder. Around their stone in the columbarium wall, I noticed a few additions—more recent deaths and their monuments. I took a moment to read the names of the new arrivals and hold their families in my thoughts. As always, when I arrived in front of my boys' place in this wall, I knelt, pressed my hand to the stone and breathed *hello.*

I'm sorry I haven't been here in so long, my loves. I left town. I needed a break. I think of you all the time and wish just as often that I could come here easily. I miss being this close to your ashes and this sacred place.

When we chose to put your ashes into urns and into the cubbyhole of this place, I felt relieved that it was something we could undo—as opposed to ashes scattered or buried in the earth. It was comforting to know we could have this gravestone removed, reach into the shelf and hold the receptacles in our hands again, should we choose. What if I wanted your ashes at home again? What if I wanted to see and hold them, even briefly? What if I moved somewhere else and needed to take you with me?

There is so much I don't feel ready for. I'm moving to Toronto because I'm not ready to come back, but I'm also not ready to stay there. I could take you with me, but I'm not ready to make that choice, either. This spot has become so imbued with memory. I realize now in the power of coming back to it, that I would grieve losing this place. I don't know how to leave you, and at the same time, I am trying hard to have a future without you.

The apartment in Vancouver was not as I'd left it, thank goodness. The subletters had changed the space to suit their needs and put more of my things into the closets and storage. That made undoing it easier to approach. My task now, motivated by the cost of moving being based on weight, was to sort through my life's belongings and decide what to carry from this point on. My childhood, my youth, every artifact was there. And of course, my life with Huz.

Being back in Vancouver was like slipping into favourite clothes. The city's streets welcomed me, and I moved easily along them. There was no energy required to navigate the place, and I clocked the lack of effort like surplus energy. Everywhere I turned, every friend I saw, I relaxed into the view. And I luxuriated in the recognition after a year of anonymity. My mom was here, cousins, friends I'd known my entire adult life; enormous pieces in a life puzzle. I'd missed these people enough that the painful reminders the place contained were less present at first.

Huz and I met at a coffee shop near the courthouse; we needed to go in person to file the last of our divorce paperwork, a process we'd started over email while I was away. He looked different; I looked different. I cried; he stiffened.

"I hope you're going to be okay someday," he said.

"It's okay to cry," I said.

At the courthouse, there was no line, and we signed where the clerk pointed, serious and tense as she turned and stamped pages.

"Congratulations, you're married!" she announced. Both Huz and I stuttered, "What?" just as she burst out laughing.

"Just kidding," she said. "You're divorced." She was still laughing as we walked away, and we started to laugh too, briefly united by the unexpected levity.

"Can we talk?" I asked outside in the spring sunshine. "Like on their birthdays, or anniversaries ..." He looked away, and I remembered all the times I'd asked him for something he couldn't give.

"It's too hard," he said.

"It's because it's hard that I wish we could talk," I said.

"You can write, if you want, but I can't say that I'll answer." We hugged goodbye, wished each other well and meant it.

The work of packing up continued: a massive yard sale, multiple trips with donations to the thrift store, friends helping me sort through closets and suitcases, often getting increasingly drunk as we progressed. Finally the movers arrived, and my life was loaded out of my East Van home in boxes. "See you in a month," I said to the last of my things, and turned around to clean the emptied apartment. In truth, my mom did most of the work, lovingly letting me wander from room to room feeling a mix of resistance and readiness.

My flight to Toronto wouldn't cross directly over the moving truck's route, but I imagined it on a highway below the clouds. I thought of everything I'd sold and given away. I thought of every loss until then; what I hadn't lost, I was leaving behind. I hummed a new song under my breath.

SEPARATION/AGREEMENT

The halls are neatly lined with boxes stacked
This is what eight years looks like packed

It's difficult to know how to decide
Which ghosts are yours and which are mine
The house has never seemed heavier than this
Even for all the empty rooms and the stillness
I'm a little bit lost here, I admit
But when I whispered your name to come back
I didn't mean it

Don't you cry for this
Don't you cry for the leaving
If you're gonna cry, make it for the reason
This is no one's fault

A slow and steady teasing out the past
Careful, it's a fragile artifact
And difficult to decipher when you're still hurting
Which part you're losing and which part you're learning

Nothing knows you better than these walls
And these walls would sigh if these walls could talk
They know every dark secret
Every dark moment
Every dark night
Every hard line, every oversight

Don't you cry for this
Don't you cry for the leaving
If you're gonna cry, make it for the reason
This is no one's fault

Inhale, exhale, rewire, program, practice, backfire
You're on track
It's a long road you're on now, and the origin is gone now

Don't look back
And don't you cry for this

CHAPTER 11 TRIBUTARIES

The host faced the audience. "After a series of personal losses that would flatten any normal human being—loss of a leg to cancer, loss of two children and loss of a marriage—Christa Couture picked herself up and started to make music again."

Standing in the wings at Toronto's Koerner Hall, I wasn't prepared for that intro. I'd been invited to a three-day event that featured fifty speakers on various topics, and I planned to talk about my prosthetic leg and play a couple of songs. Butterflies in my stomach always gave me a little pause before performing, but that intro stopped me in my tracks; it distilled my entire being into loss. *Is that how people see me? Am I really something not "normal"?*

"Where's Christa?" the host said, scanning the wings while the crowd stirred. In my hesitation, I was taking too long to come onstage.

"There she is."

It wasn't the first time I had encountered a (perhaps morbidly) curious, "How are you still standing?" crowd,

but I couldn't shake the words *cancer, children, marriage.*
Flatten. They hung over me as I stood on the stage.
Koerner Hall is an incredible space, used most often
for recitals of classical music. I felt like I'd pulled off a mar-
vellous trick just to be allowed there. First, I spoke about
cancer, about the luck of my survival, about the flower leg
I'd been transformed by. Next, picking up my acoustic guitar, I played my song "Hopeless Situation," introducing it,
as I always did, by saying how the platitude "there's always
hope" is inaccurate.

"There is *often* hope," I said. "Frequently, it makes sense
to be hopeful. But there truly are hopeless situations, and
when I wrote this song, I just wanted everyone to be okay
with that; to be okay with despair."

Everyone's performance was to be fifteen minutes
long; a large, red digital clock was counting down at my feet.
Putting the guitar on its stand, I stepped over to the hall's
beautiful grand piano in my beaded mukluks—a pair gifted
to me by my mother, made for her by a Cree woman before
I was born. In those mukluks, I feel grounded. I conserve
their power and wear them only onstage. That I was perhaps an imposter in that grand theatre, that the audience
might think I should be flattened, was further complicated
by the new scar on my neck. It was less than two months
since my thyroidectomy, and my singing voice had not fully
recovered. I half-talked my way through the songs, hoping
no one would notice the less musical delivery.

The clock ticking, I began my second song, "Aux
Oiseaux." It was the most hopeful piece I'd written to date,
and I played it in contrast to the first.

It may be that hope is most meaningful after hopelessness; it's earned then, or full-fledged. No light without dark sort of thing. I think of something my Toronto therapist said once: "Resilience sucks." Meaning, resilience is born of suffering. A person doesn't discover their capacity to survive until it is tested.

My fingers were gleeful on the Koerner Hall piano's keys. The words of the introduction drifted into the rafters as my voice filled the room. I belonged on that stage in that beautiful space at the stunning piano before hundreds of people. I was more than my losses—I was the light and power of music illuminating my post-apocalyptic self.

AUX OISEAUX

Closed, closed, closed
The signs on the windows they go:
"We're closed, closed, closed and you young thing
You better get home"
And I blush. Young thing, these days, not so much
I feel old, old, old
I feel the years of the world in my bones
But I'm not fussed, I know what I am and am not
I know what I can and cannot
I know what I have and I want
I want to hold, hold, hold and not have to let go
When death comes I want to say, "No"
But don't judge—I've been through a lot
I don't say that to say that you've not
I think that we've both been cut up—yes, we both have

But guess what? I'm glad that we're here in this dump
If together is all that we've got
It's enough for us not to give up
We'll go, go, go
I see us where shadows grow,
Where je suis aux oiseaux

—◆—

While living that year in England as a young musician, before everything, I'd had an astrology reading over the phone. My stepmother often had a new favourite astrologer or tarot reader, women with long hair, flowing dresses and feminine, at-least-three-syllable names like Lucretia, Serena, Cassandra. "I booked you a reading," she'd tell me in her New York accent. She'd pay for the sessions—a gift she wanted to give and was sure I'd benefit from. I preferred the readings to clothes I'd never wear. ("But purple was your favourite when you were a girl!") I'd half-bought in to the various readings over the years, especially the parts that suited my own desires, but had increasingly been dismissing them.

The landline phone in the shoebox London flat I shared with a flatmate had a long enough cord to reach all four rooms—granted, not much distance. I paced during the call, handset pinned between my chin and shoulder and base pressed against my hip. I'd occasionally spin in a circle to untangle myself from the cord as Serena did a tandem tarot-astrology reading. She was at the point of describing my long-term future when she said, "Children figure prominently for you."

I halted in front of the cupboard we called the "post-box"—something my flatmate and I had found curbside, drunk at the time, which explained her capacity to carry the very heavy piece of furniture home and up our flight of stairs.

"I can't have kids," I said. "I mean, I was told it's unlikely."

"Oh," Serena stammered. "In your chart, I see multiple children being very meaningful to you. They could be someone else's."

My disbelief was suspended in that moment, and Serena's stars stirred a hidden part of me. Later, after my abortion, after my Emmett died, after Ford died, I would recall her soft voice on the phone from California; did her words mean there would be more children? I wanted her to be right, though I wondered at times if "very meaningful" meant the tragedies of my children's deaths. In those years, from what I could tell, having a child meant watching them die.

At the time, in response, I picked at the peeling blue paint on the postbox and stammered myself. "Right," I said. "We'll see."

—◆—

My friend Paige had also lost a child. We'd met during our respective pregnancies—hers with her first, her daughter Mira, and mine with Emmett. Acquaintances when Mira died the day after Emmett, we became close in the months that followed. She has two living daughters now, and during her visit to Toronto, we met for dinner in a noisy vegetarian restaurant.

"I might not have another kid," I told her. Whether to try for a third child was a question I constantly debated, and one that percolated at the start of every new relationship. On every date, I thought I needed to know: Do I want to try for another or not? On this fall day, I had some peace with an imagined future where I didn't.

"Do you think I can be okay?" That was the real question. The sorrow of my losses was so present I couldn't always picture accepting my broken heart without the small repair of getting to mother a living child. Neither Paige nor I liked the word "healing." We'd discussed that before. "Healing" gets used as an absolute by too many, those who think there is an end to grief, a fix for living with sadness. Paige and I agreed there should be a better word, one that could hold the contradictions of finding joy and still carrying sorrow, a word for what helped us move forward. We used "heal" knowing we did not mean "cure."

"For me, it was having a baby," she said. "But if I hadn't, I'm sure I would have found other ways to heal. Of course, there are other ways."

Mothering had taken so many years of my life at that point, and yet I felt I had little to show for it; my children were gone. My future without more children was meaningful, I knew—it held travel and writing and friendships and unknowns. When I was ready, there would be other ways to have children in my life, perhaps through my work and certainly through developing stronger ties to my friends' kids, even though I couldn't be around small children for long without dipping into my heartache. It was difficult to see other children grow when mine did not. Any child younger than my own bewildered me; surely time must have stopped when my children died. How could other children have been born and survived? What was it about them, about their parents, that had escaped the end of the world?

After Emmett's birth and death, during Ford's life and intensely after his death, I could not look at a baby and not be overwhelmed by missing my two. Sometimes, I resented living babies—those of strangers whose lives I could easily assume were without challenge—and was ashamed of that feeling instantly. No baby, or parent, deserved my bitterness. Some friends I'd lost over the years when they could not accept me distancing myself from their children; the friendships that had endured and strengthened had space for connection and interest outside of our respective parenting experiences. Paige was one of those friends. Susan too, always.

The pain I faced around babies could intensify into anxiety attacks. On an airplane, I crumbled into convulsions as a baby cried a few rows back. No parent has an easy time travelling with young children, and I did not want to make their journey harder. At the same time, I was transported into agony, a public sharing of my suffering that I wished I could stop or conceal.

Slowly, as time went by, I chipped away at this pain. I introduced short visits that involved kids, held a newborn for a few minutes, left either situation when it became too much. In public, it got easier to first ignore children, and then be unmoved by their presence.

My friend Aynsley's advice from years earlier echoed with relevance: my life with a baby would be beautiful and challenging, my life without would be beautiful and challenging. A future where I could enjoy being with other people's children, and where I did not have more of my own, would a good one. A future in which I tried to have another child shifted in and out of clarity. All the possibilities of loss obscured the picture. The challenge to conceive, to carry a baby to term, to have a live birth—each would be a hurdle. Trying meant being open to loss at every stage. I didn't know that I could rebuild one more time, were I to lose again.

Also, the best possible outcome of a pregnancy—bringing home a child—carried this: I would hold them in my arms and feel acutely the absence of their brothers. A baby would bring reminders of deep sorrow as well as new joy. That I didn't have to imagine—I knew.

He wasn't a good cat, or even a nice cat, most of the time. He could be; he could purr and cuddle and notice you were crying, comforting you by sitting on your chest. He would play and be playful. But too often, he would turn with no warning, grabbing your arm with all four of his limbs, holding with his claws while he bit deep into your flesh. The attacks made most people dislike him enough to ignore his sweeter moods, but I always forgave him. His mood swings were apparent from the start, and so I renamed him from Tuxedo, the name he came from the SPCA with, to Gilbert Blythe. When I said his name, I wanted it to be something that I thought of as gentle. Gilbert Blythe the cat (named after the kind fictional character—the love interest of the Anne of Green Gables books and my adolescence) had grown a little into the name over the fifteen years that he'd remained my companion. He was with me when I had the abortion. He was there when I came home from the hospital without Emmett. He was there the first time we brought Ford home, and I looked at him sternly: "Do NOT hurt the baby!" He was there as Huz and I drifted apart. He was there on the plane in my move across the country to Toronto.

There, he didn't last long. Already getting old, he got sick in his new city, too sick to survive, and I knew I would have to put him down. I couldn't bear to be the one to take him to the vet, couldn't bear to be with another death. My friend Lauren took him while I sobbed across town in my apartment. With the death of my grumpy old cat went the one consistent living witness to all those years of loss. I was devastated.

Small griefs are tributaries of the river of loss, and I was easily swept downstream. The ocean is an easy metaphor for pain. At its edge, I have often felt that I can dip a toe or even wade waist-high into my sadness, but the undertow is threatening. I find it hard to be just a little wet with grief. I'm so afraid I'll be pulled under. I'm so afraid I will never come back to shore.

My Vancouver therapist had once asked me about this, about giving into sadness. "What's the worst that could happen?"

"I would be lost there," I said. In less metaphorical terms, I pictured myself as catatonic.

She leaned forward and said, "I would come and find you." I had no choice but to believe her; she gave me the courage to visit that shore more often.

That Gilbert had lived long enough to come to Toronto with me was a bookend in my life. I'd brought him home in Vancouver to the first apartment where I lived alone. Now

I was living alone again. That seemed tragic, but while I sat on the couch watching a dark late-March sky and testing the edges of my grief-ocean, my perspective shifted abruptly with a phone call: a friend's baby was dying. There had been an accident.

"He's gone," Tara, the mother, texted back after I let her know I'd heard the news of her son, Anagonse-baa. While I knew many bereaved parents, I'd gotten to know them all after the fact—after the deaths of their children and after the deaths of mine. I had not known it to *happen* to someone I already knew well.

There was a gathering, food, a fire. I was anxious to see Tara. With her son's death, I was reminded of what Joan Didion describes in *The Year of Magical Thinking*, of having "entered a place in which I could be seen only by those who were themselves recently bereaved." I felt it when Tara came into the room: *seen* in a way I seldom am. Relief swept into my body and then, immediately, regret. I would rather be lonely in grief, I thought, considering that understanding could only come through such utter heartbreak.

I knew what it meant to have lost Emmett and Ford, and, in some broader way, what it was to lose a child. But I couldn't know what Tara and Anagonse-baa had lost. Loss is both universal and intricately specific. A few times over the years, I'd been asked for advice on supporting a grieving parent. My experience, people assumed, would give me something to offer. But it was because of my experience that I knew this: nothing I could say would help.

"It's not that it gets easier, but it does change," I told Tara, in an offering of words despite myself. Watching her being embraced by friends, I remembered those impossible first few nights. Then the first week, the first month ... How slow and dark time is until the first year has passed, when counting becomes harder to do. How I ached, in the early days, for time to pass and yet hated that it did.

In my bereaved parents' group in Vancouver, someone described time passing as bringing them closer to their children—the closer they moved toward their own end of days, the closer they were to being with their dead children again. That works if you believe in an afterlife. I do not, though when I've considered my own death, or even wished for it, I have felt consoled that while I don't believe I'll be *with* my children, I will be *like* them. Gone. For me, time takes me further from my sons.

That night at the gathering, in the moments Tara and I shared by the fire, we cracked dark jokes about music— she, too, a songwriter—and about our lives as mothers on this side of death. Some around the fire bristled to hear us laughing; others understood we now shared a language.

I had met Anagonse-baa once before he died. Tara was presenting at a conference I was attending, and we shared a hotel room. I wanted to help her, a working single mom, and by then, I was ready to try and babysit. If I needed to zone out, I was certain I could manage a bit of child care and navigate disconnecting from the present a little at the same time.

On the first day I was with them both, and on the second, Tara woke up needing to step out for a minute. She would be back shortly—all I had to do was watch Anagonse-baa, whom she placed next to me on my bed.

The hotel room door closed, and I looked at him. He looked at me. *This is it*, I thought. *Don't look away.* Instead of steeling myself against sorrow, I softened. Gazing into his round, dark eyes, in his pure baby presence, something shifted. "Good morning," I said, the glee only a baby can elicit bubbling in my voice. He never broke his gaze; I didn't break mine. With each passing minute, hesitancy dissipated, resistance dissolved. I giggled with him and had the sensation of shadows being lifted. The shift, though a long time coming, felt effortless in the moment. Tara returned to the room. I didn't yet know what to call it, but I was changed.

Anagonse-baa had been the first baby since my own to conjure tenderness. Magical Anagonse-baa; he showed me I could make space for other children in my life. Sweet Anagonse-baa. I missed him and thought of the language his mother and I shared.

The certainty came in a sudden moment, with an ease that didn't align with how long I'd been unsure. I was ready to try and have a baby, and I would do so on my own.

Disappointment seemed the likelier outcome, but at least I would move forward knowing the question I'd long debated had been answered with an attempt. I was much more prepared for an intrauterine insemination (also known as artificial insemination) with donor sperm to be unsuccessful than I was for it to take. I went for my first IUI of three—I had decided in advance on a maximum—with that mindset.

A blood test two weeks after the procedure would give me the results, but a few days before then, I woke recalling my first pregnancy. *Something is different.* I walked into my living room, looking for what was out of place, and into the kitchen, scanning the counters for evidence, the question growing: what if trying worked? In the bathroom, I rummaged through drawers and found a pregnancy test from I didn't know when, possibly expired. I decided to use it anyway.

The very faint result: positive. I messaged Susan. "Could it be wrong?"

"False negatives are common. False positives aren't possible, I don't think," she wrote back. "Do you want to call?"

But I couldn't speak. To say anything out loud, even to make a move, seemed dangerous; as if to break the silence would, too, break possibility; as if I were dreaming and hoping not to wake. I moved carefully through the next few days, awaiting confirmation. Three days after, a blood test. I listened to a voice message from the fertility clinic: "Good news, Christa!"

Yes, I know.

—◆—

Toronto had been so slow to become home, in part from having to move almost comically often—expired sublets, unexpected building renovations, a landlord's family needs. Three years in, I hadn't lived anywhere longer than six months. In each new place, one of the first tasks of unpacking was to hang photos of my sons. The best location was always one I could easily look at but could also avoid if I wanted to.

There I was in my eighth home, five months pregnant, surrounded by boxes and taking the usual look around for where I would hang the pictures. I chose a spot around a corner, a place I would walk past often but also a place where

I could deliberately stop to look at them. I hammered the nails and tenderly, slowly, hung the frames. I stepped back to look at their positions and study, as I had many times, the faces of my two sons. And as so many times before, I cried. I missed them.

In that moment, my unborn child kicked in my womb, and I placed my hand on my belly to feel her movements from outside and in. I was comforted by her newness, her perfect unknowing and life's insistent continuance.

CHAPTER 12 HOW TO LOSE
EVERYTHING

Emmett's ninth birthday was approaching, and as was my custom, I decided to knit a small toy for him. The occasion is so fraught, and the annual knitting routine alleviated some of the strain. That year, though, I started to consider how the gift would be received. What nine-year-old would want a tiny hand-knit bunny?

I looked at the half-formed creation in my hands and stopped knitting. I felt foolish and sad at the reminder that I did not know who my son would have been, nor how he would want to celebrate his birthday. My hands trembled, and I shuddered into tears. Looking around the room, I remembered to take a deep breath. I remembered not to fight or damn my sorrow or my regret. I remembered not to hurry my way through crying, for unread pages of grief will simply wait until I next lay eyes on them. There is no skipping ahead. I exhaled with a snotty, grumbly sob, I blew my nose and picked up my knitting again. There was meaning, here, in my hands moving, in this moment.

·

My therapist and I disagreed: he drew a chart of grief, an arc, pointed to the end and asked, "When is this?"

"Never," I said. We were talking about my grief for my sons, and I argued I would always grieve them. He countered grief is an emotion that, like other emotions, will run its course and fade. Perhaps what I want is unattainable: a balance of living with grief without being forever crushed by it. I don't need my grief to disappear, and I don't consider grief to be negative. I have cherished, still cherish grief, and I wrote:

> *In the soil I was planted, in the sun I took for granted*
> *My roots and stem were severed from each other*
> *My waking is to weep, my comfort is to sleep*
> *But I'm not lonely here, for loss became my lover*
> *She is charming and disarming and she likes to dance*
> *Around the garden of my floundering family tree*
> *My love for her is something no one seems to understand*
> *What are we? Are we artists, here?*

Grief has slowly become integrated into my body and my art. Sometimes it still hurts enough that I gasp for air. Less often, grief curls me into a ball and renders me blind to anything outside of my shape. Other times, it moves into my chest as a wave, and with my hand to my heart and a deep breath, I sway with it until the intensity passes.

The end point on the chart of grief is, for me, the beginning of knowing how to live with it; the understanding that the intensity passes and will return and pass again.

·

Two therapists have been vital in the years since Emmett and Ford died, one in Vancouver, one in Toronto. When I was on my way to meet the first, the friend who referred me said, "Don't look at her photo beforehand."

"Why?" I asked.

"She's too beautiful."

She was beautiful, with large blue eyes and a warm laugh, a gentle and confident voice, and impeccable style— over five years, I never encountered a version of her that didn't at least *look* entirely and effortlessly together. I treasured the moment during one of our first sessions when she opened a cupboard door in her office to toss in an empty coffee cup, and a stack of other empty cups tumbled out of an overflowing recycling bin.

"So human!" she said with her lovely laugh as she stuffed them back in and got the cupboard door closed again. Her style and beauty became parts of a person who shared her human quirks often enough for me to like as well as trust her. Also, importantly, she had experienced her own losses in having children; I needed that common ground. She cried, a few times, in sessions, carefully dabbing the side of her eyes to not smudge her makeup.

"I am a feeling therapist, it's true," she said, apologizing. "But I don't usually cry." I appreciated that she did; it seemed the right response.

Of crying, during a week at least a year after Emmett's death, I found myself falling apart like in the first days. In the grocery store, in the car, at work, I was overcome.

"I thought I was better, I'm not doing any better, I'm just crying all the time!" I said to her. She nodded, held my gaze, a place I am always calmed in.

"There is simply a lot of crying to do," she said, slightly shrugging. *So human*, I remembered.

"But I feel like I'm going in circles," I said.

"You will go in circles, until you don't," she said. This too became a beacon. A reminder that there will be change in the future I can't yet predict. This I can rely on.

I'm at the hospital for an appointment that is just chiropractic—nothing diagnostic. I am not waiting for news. The chiropractor's office happens to be here, tucked away in a quiet corner that feels more like an office building than a hospital. It's taken time to find practitioners I like in Toronto; part of the energy it takes to live somewhere new is collecting favourite coffee shops, a dentist you trust, a hairdresser who gets you, all the pieces that make up peripheral relationships and routine. My long-term post-cancer care involves a small village of specialists—I don't always have options about who I get to see. When I can make choices, I am particular. This chiropractor is worth seeing in a hospital, even though hospitals are places I try to avoid.

I'm early, so I grab a coffee in the atrium, where fast food places line the half-city-block area. An atrium, by definition, is open to the sky or skylight covered. An atrium is also the upper chamber of the heart, and I can't think of those spaces without thinking of the hole in my son Ford's heart.

It's a number of years since he lived in hospitals, decades since I did too, during chemotherapy. I'm getting a coffee, and it's going to be a bad coffee, likely cold or bitter, a state of coffee that hospital food courts seem unable to escape.

When Ford was in hospital, for twelve of his fourteen months, we ate at least one and sometimes two meals a day in hospital food courts. We became experts on which food selections were the least tasteless and most affordable. In Toronto, where Ford had his longest hospital stay, we had the routine down pat. Huz and I would meet in the food court; whichever of us had left the apartment last that morning would have grabbed the free daily *Metro* paper. We'd pick up one of our usual meals and sit doing the crossword together. The *Metro* crosswords had simple questions and common pop culture references; completing them was one of our few acts of empowerment. And it was one thing the two of us could do on our own together. We knew the SickKids food court as intimately as our own kitchen, but that familiarity could never make us feel at home.

As a kid in hospital, I never left the ward. I wasn't old enough, like some of the teens, to get to wander, or well enough to walk beyond my ward without family. The rare occasion that I got to go to the cafeteria was a treat: you could order anything you wanted off the menu, as opposed to the few daily options for food delivered to your room. Any corner of the hospital outside of the ward was an adventure, even when I was being wheeled off for a test. The double doors would swing open, and as the porter pushed me towards the elevator, I'd feel a small thrill.

While on chemotherapy, I was often too sick to read or draw, so I passed the time with my collection data games:

How many ceiling tiles were there, and which portion had been chipped? How many pink triangles on the hospital bed curtain? If the room had a window to the outside world, cars provided a great opportunity for statistics–colours, frequency, time of day. As a parent sitting next to my son's bed, I read. I read with increasing voraciousness, the speed at which I completed books accelerating as the weeks went by. A friend delivered a stack of them and was caught off guard when I called and asked for more.

"More books? Already?"

Ford got sicker, and I read faster. I can't remember much about those books now. After he died, I couldn't finish any book I started. For years, I would read to the last two or three pages and then close the book for good. I had read so many books when he was alive; leaving one unfinished somehow paid respect to the emptiness I endured with him gone. And I didn't want any more endings.

Hospital food courts have zero ambiance, and they all look the same. The fake plants that flank one are like those that border every other public hospital space I've seen in Canada. Families stare bleary-eyed into coffee cups while staff members move purposefully around them on their lunch breaks.

I'm getting a coffee, and I'm flooded with memories of the hours I've spent in these spaces. The hours spent taking a break from the bedside that wasn't a break at all. The hours when I had to eat though didn't want to leave my son's bedside. The hours when I had to go back to hospital rooms but didn't want to return. The hours of killing time while waiting for a surgery to end or test results to arrive. The hours of being stuck there. Fake plants. Constant fluorescent light. Stale air. Busyness and motionlessness at once. Agonizing hours.

A young man lines up behind me. He's wearing pajamas and has a capped IV in his arm, a hospital ID bracelet on his wrist. Headphones in, he's listening to music. We make eye contact and smile. I wonder how long he's been here and how much longer he must stay.

The man who hands me my bad coffee is cheerful, and I wonder how adept he is at responding to the various moods he must encounter at this kiosk. Hospitals are all hellos and goodbyes, all anticipation and suspension, hope and accomplishment, reality and despair. He must see the gamut in the faces of those ordering greasy breakfast bagels and wilted garden salads.

I'm just here for my chiropractic appointment, but I start to cry. I look at the young man in pajama bottoms, I look at the man who's now handing me my change, and they both smile again.

I want to say: *It's not sad now, but it was so sad then.*

━━◆━━

How to lose everything: a field guide.

This is what I know—first, your heart will break. You will lose a partner, a sibling, a parent, a child, your health, your home, your work, your voice.

You will start by staying in bed—being awake is the first and hardest thing to get through, and you may ache every minute of the hours in between the relief of sleep. The ache will overwhelm you at times. The ache will press on your chest so hard it might be difficult to move. The ache will shake through your body in uncontrollable sobs. The ache will numb you to all feeling. The ache will want to break things. The ache won't care what does break.

Try to wait.

The early days of shock need to pass. Fill those days and waking hours with something, anything—it doesn't matter what, as you probably won't remember. If you can, find something that doesn't hurt you or others. That might not be possible. I recommend hours of serialized television. Seven seasons of *something*. Don't worry if you don't move from the couch or your bed.

Wait.

I enrolled in a semester at a community college, and the pretense and disconnect of being a student for part of my days was a relief. I don't remember what I studied. I remember only that I passed the time. I played the online computer game *World of Warcraft* for tens of hours every week for a year and then stopped. The other players online knew only my blood elf mage avatar, Vannawheat. The fantasy, and the task of the game, passed the time. I took a job filing tax returns. It was methodical and repetitive, and I made small talk with my co-workers. Two months later, I quit—it had passed the time.

Forgive yourself. *I forgive my resentment, I forgive my jealousy, I forgive my bitterness, I forgive my immobility, I forgive my indecision.*

Remember that disconnection can protect you when you need it, and joy is not a denial of your loss. Eventually, being awake won't hurt as much. This may be months later, or a year, two years. But one day, you will be awake, and it will be okay. For moments. And then for hours. I can't tell you that it will get easier, but you will adapt. You will get used to this loss, and you will find ways around it and with it. Some forms of grief will run their course. Some will never leave you. Some days, when grief comes toward you as a wave, you will have to stand still and let the impact roll into your body and there will be no choice but to welcome its presence. Some days, you will see grief coming, and you will be able to say, "Now is not a good time." And it will listen. Sorrow can be a stubborn friend, but also a patient one. Know that sorrow evolved from joy—that she knows and remembers happiness as well as she understands where tears come from.

For that, sorrow is a powerful and wise emotion, and you will be wiser with her. You will be tender in new spots and harder in others. You won't be the same person as before—I'm sorry, that, too, is a loss. I will not tell you that which doesn't kill us makes us stronger. I will not tell you your loss is for the better. You will lose everything, and it will be different.

Remember: you have the right to honour. To honour the memory of the person, place, time and potential you lost. To remember, as often as you need, what you love, what you miss, what still brings you joy, what still hurts your heart.

And—you have the right to forget. Truly. The most painful memories are yours to let go of, when you're ready. You are not dishonouring those memories by letting them go. Trust me. If you like, find a place for them, for safekeeping. Tell a person close to you and let them know you are telling them this story for them to remember and you to forget. Write a letter and drop it, unaddressed, in a mailbox or into the flames of a fire or under a mound of dirt at the base of a tree. Walk into the woods, dig a hole and cry or sing or sob or tell your most painful memory into the earth.

Or tell me. Tell me right now to this page, and I will remember for you. I will remember the name of your child. I will remember the laugh of your sister. I will remember the place where your home stood—just as you will remember these pages for me.

ACKNOWLEDGEMENTS

I gratefully acknowledge funding support from the Ontario Arts Council, an agency of the Government of Ontario, and the Canada Council for the Arts. This manuscript was produced with the support of the City of Toronto through the Toronto Arts Council.

How to Lose Everything is a work of nonfiction, though some names and descriptive details have been changed.

Earlier versions of the chapters "These Are My Children," "Sanibe" and "Shapeshifter" appeared in *The M Word: Conversations about Motherhood* (Goose Lane, 2014), *Radiant Voices: 21 Feminist Essays for Rising Up Inspired by EMMA Talks* (TouchWood Editions, 2019) and *Room Magazine* (2014), respectively.

There are so many to thank:

Kerry Clare, for asking me to write a small thing that led to this big thing, and for connecting the dots to Sam Haywood and my agent, Stephanie Sinclair. Sam, for her faith and passion and for inspiring a shift from writing a different book into writing this one. Stephanie, for her conviction, after-bedtime help and guidance that never settled for less than excellent.

Wayne Grady and my cohort at the 2016 Emerging Writers Intensive for nourishing this book's earliest stages; Nancy Holmes, who instilled confidence in its tender roots; and Bill Richardson, whose words of encouragement were taped to my wall throughout.

Michele Kambolis, for finding me in the dark. Carlos Rivas, for being the first to tell me, "You have the right to honour and to forget."

Caterina Edwards, for being the first to read a complete draft and whose feedback ensured the second was a cut above.

Susan Kendal, for being my Lou all these years, and for spending a day at her dining table painstakingly turning pages of that draft by my side.

Barbara Pulling, for her care, precision, encouragement and insight as editor.

Anna Comfort O'Keeffe and all at Douglas & McIntyre, for their enthusiasm, faith and support.

The friends and family who have, over these years, caught me from below and sheltered me from above: Christine, Jean-Guy, Myia, David, Jennifer-Lynn, Tara Rhae, Mike, Diederik, Paige, Aynsley, Angela, Nick and Nick's family, Ruth, Kathleen, Kendals and Urbachs, and my mom.

Marsha Shandur, whose cheerleading, calendar shuffling and love made this book possible above all else.

Sona, who grounded me enough in the present that I could look back at it all. Aren't we lucky, little one.

Download or stream all of the songs mentioned in *How to Lose Everything* at christacouture.com/everything-music